VEGETARIAN PÂTÉS & DIPS

A wealth of appetizing wholefood dishes to suit all tastes and occasions.

vegetarian PÂTÉS & DIPS

For Parties, First Courses, Quick Lunches or Late Night Snacks

by

JANET HUNT

Illustrated by Kim Blundell

THORSONS PUBLISHING GROUP
Wellingborough, Northamptonshire

Rochester, Vermont

First published January 1986
Second Impression July 1986

British Library Cataloguing in Publication Data

Hunt, Janet
  Vegetarian pâtés and dips: for parties, first courses,
  quick lunches or late night snacks.
  1. Vegetarian cookery   2. Cookery (Appetizers)
  I. Title
  641.8'12   TX837

ISBN 0-7225-1191-4

Printed in Great Britain by
Richard Clay (The Chaucer Press) Ltd,
Bungay, Suffolk

CONTENTS

		Page
Introduction		7
Chapter		
1.	Everyday Pâtés	13
2.	Party Pâtés	32
3.	Cold Dips	50
4.	Hot Dips	70
5.	Mousses and Moulds	76
6.	Accompaniments	90
	Appendix: Menu Ideas	107
	Index	111

INTRODUCTION

It's a rare party at which pâtés and dips, of one kind or another, don't put in an appearance. They are classic party fare: easy to eat even when you are standing, tasty, and — best of all — able to be prepared well in advance so that there are no last minute panics. For the same reasons they are often used to get a dinner party off to a good start.

But because of this party image, they are not served anywhere near as often as they could and should be. Dips, for example, make ideal and health conscious nibbles for between-meal or late-night hunger pangs. If chosen carefully, and dipped into with carrot and celery sticks, they will also be popular with dieters. Or they can double as the most delicious and unusual salad dressings, many of them protein-rich too. It is well worth keeping one or two made-up dips ready in the fridge — in the unlikely event that they are still around a day or two later, they can be stirred into soups or casseroles.

Pâtés make a snack lunch that bit more special. Serve them with wholemeal bread or baps, or fresh French bread, add a simple salad, and you have an instant meal that will be nutritionally balanced as well as good to eat. Because they spread well, pâtés also make excellent sandwich fillings. The word *pâté* comes from the French, and originally referred to the pastry case in which various savoury ingredients were wrapped and served. *Pâté en croute*, then, is a pâté in a flaky pastry, and can be a meal in itself. *Vol-au-vents* too are delicious when filled with pâté, especially if served whilst still warm.

A more unusual way of using pâtés is as a filling for vegetables. Raw tomatoes, celery sticks, cucumber and courgette 'boats', blanched pepper halves — all can be stuffed with pâtés and served on those occasions that demand a little extra effort, such as a special summer buffet, or the first course of a dinner party.

One of the things that makes pâtés unpopular with vegetarians is that they are almost always based on minced or pounded game, liver, poultry, meat or fish. *Pâté de foie gras*, probably the best known of all, is made from the extended livers of geese that are force-fed on maize until they are in danger of dying of heart attacks, and must be slaughtered quickly — a production method that surely must leave a nasty taste in the mouth of anyone who has any feelings at all. Such pâtés also tend to be high in calories and saturated fats, a problem not helped by the traditional method of enriching them with lashings of thick cream or butter.

The recipes in this book aim to offer alternatives. They include everyday pâtés made from less expensive ingredients, produced in next to no time. There are pâtés for when you want to serve something rather special — *terrines*, for example, a name that once referred to the earthenware dish in which pâtés were both cooked and served, but which has now come to mean pâtés in which the ingredients are layered for attractive visual effects. There are, in fact, pâtés for all tastes, pockets and occasions. As most of them will keep for up to a week in the fridge (and will even improve in flavour), they can be made when you have time to spare, making them very convenient.

There is also a selection of dips, cold ones for hot summer days, hot dips and fondues for winter, most of which can be prepared without special equipment. Another idea for parties, a first course at dinner, or a light and refreshing summer lunch, is mousses and savoury jellies; usually based on gelatine, the recipes given here are made with agaragar. To accompany all of these you will find a selection of biscuits, breads, croûtons and vegetables.

Choosing Ingredients

All of these are based on wholefoods, ingredients that can be bought at your greengrocers and the local wholefood or health food shop. It is worth paying that little extra for items such as free range eggs, organically grown vegetables whenever they are available, genuine tamari soya sauce, fresh nuts and cheeses. Though butter is usually used in traditional pâtés, polyunsaturated margarine is suggested in most of the following recipes, except where it might diminish the flavour of the finished dish. In fact, butter does have a place in a wholefood diet as it is a more natural product than most margarines. Besides, unlike more meat-based pâtés, these ones are low in saturated fats, and can therefore afford the luxury of a little butter without becoming too rich for most people's tastes and too clogging for their arteries!

When seasoning any of the following dishes, use freshly ground black pepper. Sea salt has always been considered to be best, and certainly has many trace minerals, including iodine. However, as the seas become increasingly polluted, rock salts are being suggested as a better choice. Either way keep salt intake to a minimum. Herbs can be fresh or dried, and though types and quantities have been specified, be adventurous — use the types you like best or have readily available and in the amounts that you and your family prefer.

By their very nature pâtés, dips and mousses tend to be based on, or include dairy products such as cheese, cream, yogurt and soured cream. This gives them the texture for which they are known and usually much enjoyed. This does, however, make many of them unsuitable for vegans. There are still a number of recipes which vegans may enjoy in the following pages, and others that can be adapted without too much effort. A number of soya 'milks' and 'creams' are now available, which can be substituted for the real thing. Tofu is also ideal, and tahini can be used in limited amounts to add creaminess. When making pâtés, try them with ground beans, nuts or cooked grains to add bulk. Creamed coconut adds taste as it thickens, and goes well with many ingredients, vegetables especially. Mashed potato can also be added to a pâté, and if used with a knob or two of vegan margarine, is also a good substitute for cream.

Equipment You Will Need

Making pâtés, dips and savoury jellies can be as simple or complicated a task as you choose to make it. There are now numerous foods processors on the market that grind, blend, purée, whip, crush, drain — do just about everything for you. These obviously do take much of the work out of preparing all kinds of dishes, and if you have one, by all means use it to produce the recipes in this book. As each food processor will vary in abilities and methods of use, follow the instructions that come with your particular model.

A simpler and far less expensive piece of equipment is an electric blender/grinder. This usually consists of a small grinder (excellent for nuts, beans, etc. as well as coffee) with an attachment that slips over the top. One problem with such a blender is that liquid needs to be added to make the blades able to work, and although this is fine for dips, pâtés are generally drier and more firm in texture, and the ingredients must not get too wet. If using such a machine, add the absolute minimum of liquid (if not specified in the recipe, use water, vegetable stock, dairy or soya milk or cream, as appropriate). When smooth the mixture may need to be thickened with a little wheatgerm, breadcrumbs, bran or soya flour.

There are still many cooks who do not have, nor even want, all the latest mod cons for their kitchens. They may get great pleasure from mixing, mashing, chopping by hand, seeing this as a part of the experience of cooking, to be enjoyed rather than suffered as a duty or a task. They may prefer peace to the sharp buzz of electric gadgets. For such people, a mortar and pestle is ideal for grinding the softer ingredients. A sieve can also be used to break down some foods, as can a small hand grinder, or even a grater. Items such as nuts can be put between two sheets of clingfilm and crushed with a rolling pin — they won't be as fine as if ground, but will give an interesting coarser texture to a dish. A hand whisk, used to make a dip, will lighten as it mixes. And for those who have only the very minimum of equipment, a sharp knife, a chopping block, and a strong fork can work wonders.

Presentation of food will also make a huge difference to how much it is enjoyed. For pâtés you will need either an attractive medium-sized dish which can be passed around for everyone to help themselves, or small individual sized ramekins, one for each person. Pâtés with especially firm textures, such as those that have been cooked, can be carefully tipped out onto a flat plate, garnished, and then cut into slices at the table. Terrines in particular are impressive served this way. However, if cooked in a table-worthy earthenware dish (rather than a loaf tin, which makes an excellent if mundane alternative), simply chill the pâté or terrine in the same dish, and serve it straight from the fridge. Other unusual containers for pâtés include avocado shells, nests of crisp lettuce, artichoke shells, and so on, depending on the powers of your imagination.

Dips can be presented in any small dishes or bowls. Choose them carefully: if the dip is pale in colour, try to counteract this with a more interesting shade or texture in the container (though you can always, of course, add interest with a garnish). Melba toast and other bread or biscuit accompaniments for dipping look good in a small straw basket lined with a coloured napkin.

The recipes given in this book are only meant to be a starting point — go on and experiment with combinations of your own. There are no rules in cooking, no rights and wrongs. Use natural, wholesome ingredients plus your own imagination, and though your pâtés, dips and mousses may be nothing like the traditional kind, they will still make very good eating.

Quantities given will serve 3-6 people, depending on how they are being served.

1.
EVERYDAY PÂTÉS

CURRIED SPLIT PEA PÂTÉ

Imperial (Metric)
4 oz (115g) dried split peas, soaked
   overnight
1 oz (30g) polyunsaturated
   margarine or ghee
1 large onion, chopped
2 teaspoons curry powder
4 oz (115g) low-fat soft cheese
Cucumber slices to garnish

American
½ cup dried split peas, soaked
   overnight
2½ tablespoons polyunsaturated
   margarine or ghee
1 large onion, chopped
2 teaspoons curry powder
½ cup low-fat soft cheese
Cucumber slices to garnish

1. Put the split peas in fresh water, bring to the boil and continue boiling for 10 minutes. Then lower the heat, cover pan, and cook for approximately 1 hour until peas are soft.

2. Melt the fat and fry the chopped onion to soften.

3. Sprinkle in the curry powder and cook gently a few minutes more.

4. Drain the peas very well and stir into the onion mixture. Set aside to cool.

5. In a blender, make a thick purée of the peas.

6. Stir in the cheese, making sure it is well blended.

7. Transfer to a small dish, smooth the top, and chill the pâté. Serve garnished with thin rings of cucumber.

OAT AND PARSNIP PÂTÉ

Imperial (Metric)	American
1 lb (455g) parnips	1 pound parnips
1 large onion	1 large onion
1 oz (30g) polyunsaturated margarine	2½ tablespoons polyunsaturated margarine
Approximately ¼ pint (140ml) water or vegetable stock	Approximately ⅔ cup water or vegetable stock
2 oz (55g) rolled oats	½ cup rolled oats
4 oz (115g) Cheddar cheese, grated	1 cup Cheddar cheese, grated
1 teaspoon dried basil	1 teaspoon dried basil
Seasoning to taste	Seasoning to taste
1-2 tablespoons double cream (optional)	1-2 tablespoons heavy cream (optional)
Parsley to garnish	Parsley to garnish

1. Peel and chop the parsnips and onion.

2. Melt the margarine, add the vegetables, and cook gently for 5 minutes, stirring occasionally.

3. Add the vegetable stock and cook the vegetables for 5 minutes more. Stir in the rolled oats and cook briefly to make a mush-like mixture.

4. Add the grated cheese whilst the mixture is still warm; flavour with basil and seasoning.

5. Blend to make a thick, smooth paste. Adjust seasoning. Stir in the cream if desired.

6. Transfer the pâté to a serving dish and chill well. Garnish with fresh parsley sprigs.

EGG AND AVOCADO PÂTÉ

Imperial (Metric)	American
2 medium-sized ripe avocados	2 medium-sized ripe avocados
1 tablespoon lemon juice	1 tablespoon lemon juice
1 large tomato	1 large tomato
2 spring onions	2 scallions
3 hard-boiled eggs	3 hard-boiled eggs
1-2 tablespoons mayonnaise	1-2 tablespoons mayonnaise
Seasoning to taste	Seasoning to taste
Strips of red pepper to garnish	Strips of red pepper to garnish

1. Peel and mash the avocados together with the lemon juice.

2. Scald the tomato in boiling water, and then remove the skin and chop the flesh. Finely chop the onions, mash the eggs, and mix into the avocados with the tomato, and just enough mayonnaise to give the pâté a creamy texture.

3. Season to taste, turn the mixture into a small dish, and chill well.

4. Garnish with attractively arranged strips of red pepper before serving.

QUICK PEANUT PÂTÉ

Imperial (Metric)	**American**
4 tablespoons smooth peanut butter	4 tablespoons smooth peanut butter
4 oz (115g) Ricotta cheese	½ cup Ricotta cheese
Garlic salt	Garlic salt
½ teaspoon oregano, or to taste	½ teaspoon oregano, or to taste
Seasoning to taste	Seasoning to taste
1 teaspoon chopped spring onion *or* chives to garnish	1 teaspoon chopped scallion *or* chives to garnish

1. Mash the peanut butter until smooth and soft, then mix with the Ricotta cheese.

2. Add the flavourings and beat well so that all the ingredients are thoroughly blended.

3. Transfer to a serving dish, smooth the top, and chill well. Serve garnished with chopped onion or chives.

KIDNEY BEAN PÂTÉ

Imperial (Metric)
6 oz (170g) kidney beans, soaked overnight
2 oz (55g) polyunsaturated margarine
2 spring onions, finely chopped
1 small green pepper, chopped
½-1 clove garlic, crushed
1 teaspoon paprika, or to taste
1 teaspoon cayenne, or to taste
Seasoning to taste
¼ pint (140ml) soured cream
Soya 'bacon' bits to garnish

American
1 cup kidney beans, soaked overnight
¼ cup polyunsaturated margarine
2 scallions, finely chopped
1 small green pepper, chopped
½-1 clove garlic, crushed
1 teaspoon paprika, or to taste
1 teaspoon cayenne, or to taste
Seasoning to taste
⅔ cup soured cream
Soy *Bac-O-Bits* to garnish

1. Put the beans in fresh water and then boil them vigorously for 10 minutes. Cover the pan and simmer for 50 minutes more, or until the beans are tender. Drain well and set aside.

2. Melt the margarine and cook the finely chopped onions, green pepper and the garlic until soft. Add the spices and cook a minute more.

3. Mash the beans and mix them into the cooked vegetables, making a thick even paste. Season to taste and leave to cool.

4. Stir in the soured cream.

5. Transfer the pâté to a small bowl, cover and chill well. Serve garnished with 'bacon' bits.

CAULIFLOWER AND RED LENTIL PÂTÉ

nothing special

Imperial (Metric)
6 oz (170g) split red lentils
1 medium cauliflower
2 tablespoons vegetable oil
1 small onion, finely chopped
1 oz (30g) wholemeal flour
Seasoning to taste
½-1 teaspoon yeast extract
Approximately ½ teaspoon marjoram
Tomato to garnish

American
¾ cup split red lentils
1 medium cauliflower
2 tablespoons vegetable oil
1 small onion, finely chopped
¼ cup wholewheat flour
Seasoning to taste
½-1 teaspoon yeast extract
Approximately ½ teaspoon marjoram
Tomato to garnish

1. Cover the lentils with water, bring to a boil, then simmer for 15-20 minutes or until soft.

2. Break the cauliflower into florets and steam well. Reserve the water.

3. In a clean pan heat the oil and fry the finely chopped onion until it begins to colour.

4. Sprinkle the flour over the onion, stir, and cook a minute or two more.

5. Pour in about ¼ pint (140ml/⅔ cup) of the vegetable water and cook to make a thick sauce.

6. Mash the lentils and the cauliflower, and add them to the sauce, stirring well. Add seasoning, yeast extract and marjoram.

7. Transfer the ingredients to a serving dish. Chill briefly before serving. Garnish with slices of tomato.

CHEESE PÂTÉ WITH OLIVES

Imperial (Metric)	American
1 oz (30g) polyunsaturated margarine	2½ tablespoons polyunsaturated margarine
1 oz (30g) wholemeal flour	¼ cup wholewheat flour
¼ pint (140ml) milk	⅔ cup milk
4 oz (115g) grated Cheddar cheese	1 cup grated Cheddar cheese
1-2 tablespoons mayonnaise	1-2 tablespoons mayonnaise
Seasoning to taste	Seasoning to taste
12 stuffed olives	12 stuffed olives
Chives to garnish	Chives to garnish

1. Melt the margarine in a saucepan, sprinkle in the wholemeal flour, and cook gently for a minute or two.

2. Stir in the milk and continue cooking until the sauce thickens.

3. Add the grated cheese, mix well. Set aside to cool slightly.

4. Add the mayonnaise, seasoning and chopped olives.

5. Turn the mixture into a dish, smooth the top. Chill before serving garnished with snipped chives.

WALNUT PÂTÉ

Imperial (Metric)	American
1 oz (30g) polyunsaturated margarine	2½ tablespoons polyunsaturated margarine
½ small onion, finely chopped	½ small onion, finely chopped
1 oz (30g) wholemeal flour	¼ cup wholewheat flour
Approximately ⅛ pint (70ml) water	¼ cup water
3 oz (85g) walnuts	⅔ cup English walnuts
Good squeeze of lemon juice	Good squeeze of lemon juice
2 tablespoons tomato purée	2 tablespoons tomato paste
¼ teaspoon dried thyme	¼ teaspoon dried thyme
¼ teaspoon dried basil	¼ teaspoon dried basil
1 tablespoon fresh parsley, chopped	1 tablespoon fresh parsley, chopped
Seasoning to taste	Seasoning to taste
1 tablespoon single cream *or* yogurt	1 tablespoon light cream *or* yogurt
Watercress to garnish	Watercress to garnish

1. Melt the margarine in a saucepan, and sauté the finely chopped onion for a few minutes.

2. Sprinkle in the flour and cook briefly, then stir in enough water to make a thick sauce.

3. Grind the walnuts.

4. Add the nuts, lemon juice, tomato purée (paste), herbs and seasoning to the sauce, mixing well.

5. Stir in the cream or yogurt. The mixture should be stiff, but if it is too thick, add more lemon juice, tomato purée (paste) or cream.

6. Put into a serving dish and smooth the top. Chill briefly. Garnish with watercress before serving.

SOYA YEAST PÂTÉ

Imperial (Metric)
1 oz (30g) polyunsaturated
   margarine
½ small onion, finely chopped
2 oz (55g) mushrooms, chopped
Approximately ¼ pint (140ml)
   vegetable stock
2 oz (55g) soya flakes
1 teaspoon yeast extract, or to taste
1 teaspoon tomato purée
Seasoning to taste
Chopped chives to garnish

American
2½ tablespoons polyunsaturated
   margarine
½ small onion, finely chopped
¾ cup mushrooms, chopped
Approximately ⅔ cup vegetable
   stock
4 heaped tablespoons soy flakes
1 teaspoon yeast extract, or to taste
1 teaspoon tomato paste
Seasoning to taste
Chopped chives to garnish

1. Melt the polyunsaturated margarine in a saucepan. Gently fry the chopped onion for a few minutes, then add the chopped mushrooms and continue cooking 5 minutes more, stirring occasionally.

2. Pour in the vegetable stock, add the soya (soy) flakes. Add the yeast extract and tomato purée (paste), stirring so that they dissolve. Season to taste.

3. Cook gently until all the ingredients are soft. Add a drop more liquid, if necessary.

4. Drain off any excess liquid then mash or purée or blend the remaining mixture to make a paste.

5. Transfer to a small dish, and leave to cool to room temperature. Cover and chill. Serve garnished with chopped chives.

BARLEY AND BEAN PÂTÉ

Imperial (Metric)
2 tablespoons vegetable oil
1 small onion, finely chopped
1 clove garlic, crushed
4 oz (115g) mushrooms, chopped
3 oz (85g) butter beans, soaked
  overnight
½ lb (225g) pot barley, soaked
  overnight
½ pint (285ml) vegetable stock
Fresh parsley
Seasoning to taste

American
2 tablespoons vegetable oil
1 small onion, finely chopped
1 clove garlic, crushed
1½ cups mushrooms, chopped
½ cup Lima beans, soaked overnight
1 cup pot barley, soaked overnight
1⅓ cups vegetable stock
Fresh parsley
Seasoning to taste

1. Heat the oil in a pan and sauté the finely chopped onion with the garlic until they soften.

2. Add the chopped mushrooms and cook a few minutes more.

3. Add the well drained beans and pot barley, plus the vegetable stock. Bring to a fast boil and boil for 10 minutes. Then cover the pan, lower the heat, and simmer for about 40 minutes, or until all the ingredients are well cooked.

4. Drain off the liquid. Purée or mash the ingredients to make a thick paste (add a drop of the stock if it is too dry).

5. Mix in a generous amount of chopped parsley and season to taste.

6. Transfer to a serving bowl and chill. Garnish with extra parsley before serving.

WATERCRESS EGG PÂTÉ

Imperial (Metric)
2 large hard-boiled eggs, quartered
1 bunch watercress
1 tablespoon chopped parsley
4 oz (115g) curd cheese
Milk to mix
Seasoning to taste

American
2 large hard-boiled eggs, quartered
1 bunch watercress
1 tablespoon chopped parsley
½ cup curd cheese
Milk to mix
Seasoning to taste

1. Put the quartered eggs into a blender.

2. Trim the tough stalks from the watercress, and add the leaves to the eggs together with the parsley and cheese. Blend until smooth.

3. Add enough milk to soften the mixture as necessary. Season to taste.

4. Chill the pâté well before serving.

MOCK MEAT PÂTÉ

Imperial (Metric)	American
4 oz (115g) soya minced 'beef'	1 cup soy minced 'beef'
1 oz (30g) polyunsaturated margarine	2½ tablespoons polyunsaturated margarine
1 oz (30g) wholemeal flour	¼ cup wholewheat flour
¼ pint (140ml) milk	⅔ cup milk
½ small onion, finely chopped	½ small onion, finely chopped
3 tablespoons single cream	3 tablespoons light cream
Seasoning to taste	Seasoning to taste
½ teaspoon mixed herbs	½ teaspoon mixed herbs
2 eggs, beaten	2 eggs, beaten
Lemon slices to garnish	Lemon slices to garnish

1. Hydrate the soya 'beef' in hot water. Set aside.

2. Melt the polyunsaturated margarine and sprinkle in the flour. Cook for a few minutes, then add the milk, stir well, and heat gently to make a thick sauce.

3. Add the finely chopped onion, the cream, seasoning and herbs.

4. Drain the 'beef' well, and stir it into the sauce (this can be puréed first for a smoother pâté, if you prefer). Add the beaten eggs and mix thoroughly.

5. Transfer the mixture to a lightly-greased shallow dish, preferably earthenware. Press down and level the top. Stand this in a tin containing at least 1 inch (2.5cm) of water.

6. Bake at 325°F/170°C (Gas Mark 3) for 45-55 minutes, or until set.

7. Cool the pâté, then garnish with slices of lemon.

PEA AND POTATO PÂTÉ

Imperial (Metric)	American
3 oz (85g) cooked green peas	½ cup cooked green peas
½ lb (225g) potatoes	8 ounces potatoes
4 oz (115g) curd cheese	½ cup curd cheese
¼ pint (140ml) natural yogurt	⅔ cup plain yogurt
Chopped green chilli pepper	Chopped green chili pepper
Seasoning to taste	Seasoning to taste
Fresh mint to garnish	Fresh mint to garnish

1. Drain the peas, and then press them through a sieve.

2. Peel and cube the potatoes. Steam until just tender, drain well, and set aside to cool.

3. Mash the potatoes together with the curd cheese and yogurt. Add the peas and mix well.

4. Flavour with chilli pepper (these are hot, so use sparingly). Add seasoning.

5. Turn the mixture into a bowl and chill. Serve garnished with fresh mint.

RAW VEGETABLE PÂTÉ

Imperial (Metric)	**American**
2 spring onions	2 scallions
1 large carrot	1 large carrot
1 large stick celery	1 large stalk celery
2 oz (55g) mushrooms	¾ cup mushrooms
1 teaspoon chopped parsley	1 teaspoon chopped parsley
1 teaspoon chopped basil	1 teaspoon chopped basil
1 tablespoon lemon juice	1 tablespoon lemon juice
2 egg yolks (raw)	2 egg yolks (raw)
2 oz (55g) ground mixed nuts	½ cup ground mixed nuts
1-2 tablespoons vegetable oil	1-2 tablespoons vegetable oil
Seasoning to taste	Seasoning to taste

1. With a sharp knife chop the onions (scallions), carrot, celery and mushrooms as finely as possible.

2. Put them into a bowl and mix thoroughly with the parsley, basil, lemon juice, egg yolks and nuts.

3. Add just as much oil as is necessary to bind everything together. Season well.

4. Turn into a serving dish, smooth the top, and chill briefly.

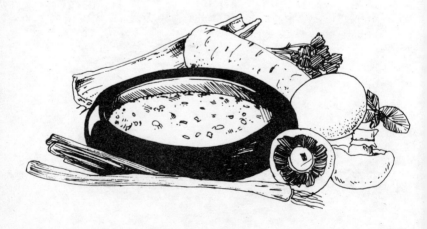

CHICK PEA PÂTÉ

Imperial (Metric)	American
6 oz (170g) chick peas, soaked overnight	¾ cup garbanzo beans, soaked overnight
2 tablespoons vegetable oil	2 tablespoons vegetable oil
1 small onion, finely chopped	1 small onion, finely chopped
1 small green pepper, chopped	1 small green pepper, chopped
1 stick celery, chopped	1 stalk celery, chopped
2 tablespoons lemon juice	2 tablespoons lemon juice
1 teaspoon dried oregano	1 teaspoon dried oregano
Seasoning to taste	Seasoning to taste
1 oz (30g) sesame seeds	1 heaped tablespoon sesame seeds

1. Drain the chick peas (garbanzos), cover with fresh water, and bring to a fast boil. Continue boiling for 10 minutes, then simmer for 1-1½ hours or until cooked. Drain.

2. In a clean saucepan heat the oil and gently sauté the finely chopped onion, pepper, and celery. When just soft, remove from heat.

3. Grind the chick peas (garbanzos) to a powder and stir into the vegetables in the saucepan, mixing thoroughly.

4. Add lemon juice, oregano and seasoning. Though the pâté should be firm in texture, you can add a little extra oil if it seems too dry.

5. Transfer to a serving dish and chill briefly. Sprinkle with sesame seeds before serving.

BRUSSELS SPROUTS PÂTÉ 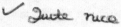 Quite nice

Imperial (Metric)
1 lb (455g) Brussels sprouts
1 onion, chopped
Approximately ½ pint (285ml)
 vegetable stock
Squeeze of lemon juice
Approximately 3 tablespoons tahini
Seasoning to taste
Approximately 1 oz (30g) wholemeal
 breadcrumbs
Red pepper rings to garnish

American
1 pound Brussels sprouts
1 onion, chopped
1⅓ cups vegetable stock
Squeeze of lemon juice
Approximately 3 tablespoons tahini
Seasoning to taste
½ cup wholewheat breadcrumbs
Red pepper rings to garnish

1. Trim, wash and slice the Brussels sprouts.

2. Put them into a saucepan with the onion, pour on the vegetable stock, and cover the pan with a lid. Simmer for about 20 minutes, checking the liquid every now and again.

3. When tender, set the sprouts aside to cool.

4. Drain them, then blend with the lemon juice and enough tahini to make a creamy purée. Season to taste.

5. Stir in the breadcrumbs to thicken. Transfer the mixture to a bowl and chill. Garnish with red pepper rings.

NUTTY SOYA PÂTÉ

Imperial (Metric)
3 oz (85g) cooked soya beans
3 oz (85g) raw peanuts
1 stick celery
½ red pepper
Seasoning to taste
Garlic salt
Soya sauce
2-3 tablespoons vegetable oil

American
½ cup cooked soy beans
⅔ cup raw peanuts
1 stalk celery
½ red pepper
Seasoning to taste
Garlic salt
Soy sauce
2-3 tablespoons vegetable oil

1. Drain the soya (soy) beans well.

2. Grind the beans to a powder. Do the same with the peanuts. Mix well together.

3. Finely chop the celery and pepper, and add to the dry ingredients with the seasoning, garlic salt and soya (soy) sauce.

4. Add enough vegetable oil to bind the mixture to a thick paste. Transfer to a small serving dish. Chill well before serving.

BLACK BEAN PÂTÉ

Imperial (Metric)	American
6 oz (170g) black beans, soaked overnight	1 cup black beans, soaked overnight
2 tablespoons vegetable oil	2 tablespoons vegetable oil
½ oz (15g) polyunsaturated margarine	1 good tablespoon polyunsaturated margarine
1 large leek, sliced	1 large leek, sliced
1 clove garlic, crushed	1 clove garlic, crushed
2 tomatoes	2 tomatoes
1 tablespoon tomato purée	1 tablespoon tomato paste
Seasoning to taste	Seasoning to taste
1 hard-boiled egg to garnish	1 hard-boiled egg to garnish

1. Drain the beans, put into fresh water, bring to the boil and continue boiling for 10 minutes. Lower the heat and cover the pan. Simmer for 45 minutes, or until the beans are tender.

2. In a clean pan, heat the oil and margarine, and lightly sauté the sliced leek with the garlic until both begin to soften.

3. Add the chopped tomatoes and tomato purée (paste), and cook 5 minutes more. Add the drained beans. Mix well.

4. Process or mash the ingredients to make a thick paste. Season to taste and stir in a generous amount of fresh chopped parsley.

5. Turn the pâté into a bowl and chill lightly. Garnish with chopped hard-boiled egg.

CREAMY CHEESE PÂTÉ

Imperial (Metric)	American
4 oz (115g) cream cheese	½ cup cream cheese
4 oz (115g) sage Lancashire cheese	1 cup sage Lancashire cheese
1-2 teaspoons crushed sage	1-2 teaspoons crushed sage
¼ small onion, grated	¼ small onion, grated
1 oz (30g) sesame seeds	1 heaped tablespoon sesame seeds
Milk to mix	Milk to mix
Seasoning to taste	Seasoning to taste
Paprika and chopped chives to garnish	Paprika and chopped chives to garnish

1. In a bowl cream together the two cheeses, the sage and finely grated onion.

2. Roast the seeds in a dry heavy-based pan, shaking it frequently. Keep the heat low. Remove after 3-5 minutes, or when golden brown.

3. Cool the seeds, then grind them to a powder and stir into the cheese mixture.

4. Add enough milk to make a thick smooth paste — it should still be firm. Season well. Spoon into a serving bowl and smooth the top. Chill well. Serve the pâté garnished with paprika and chopped chives.

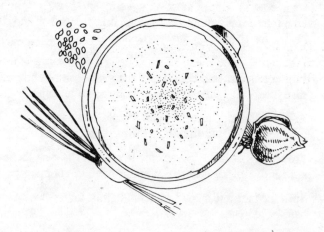

SWEET AND SOUR BEAN PÂTÉ

Imperial (Metric)
½ lb (225g) haricot or field beans,
  soaked overnight,
2 tablespoons vegetable oil
1 onion, chopped
1 green pepper, chopped

For sauce:
Scant 1 oz (30g) cornflour
1 tablespoon soya sauce
1 tablespoon dry sherry
2 oz (55g) raw cane sugar
⅛ pint (70ml) white wine vinegar
⅛ pint (70ml) vegetable stock
Parsley to garnish

American
1 cup navy or field beans, soaked
  overnight,
2 tablespoons vegetable oil
1 onion, chopped
1 green pepper, chopped

For sauce:
Scant ¼ cup cornstarch
1 tablespoon soy sauce
1 tablespoon dry sherry
⅓ cup raw cane sugar
¼ cup white wine vinegar
¼ cup vegetable stock
Parsley to garnish

1. Put the beans in a saucepan with fresh water, bring them to a boil, and continue boiling for 10 minutes. Lower the heat, cover, and cook for 45-50 minutes more, or until beans are tender.

2. Heat the oil in a clean pan and fry the chopped onion and pepper to soften.

3. Combine all the ingredients for the sauce, mixing well. Pour onto the onion and pepper mixture and stir. Simmer gently until the sauce thickens. Leave to cool slightly.

4. Drain the beans, and mash or grind them to make a purée. Add to the sauce. If too thick, adjust consistency with vegetable stock. Transfer to a dish and chill before serving. Garnish with sprigs of parsley.

2.
PARTY PÂTÉS

CELERY AND BLUE CHEESE PÂTÉ

Imperial (Metric)	American
3 large sticks celery	3 large stalks celery
4 oz (115g) blue cheese	1 cup blue cheese
4 oz (115g) Ricotta cheese	½ cup Ricotta cheese
Seasoning to taste	Seasoning to taste
Soya 'bacon' bits to garnish	Soy *Bac-O-Bits* to garnish

1. Chop the celery as fine as possible.

2. Put into a saucepan with just enough water to cover, top with a lid, and simmer the celery for 20-30 minutes, or until soft.

3. Remove the lid. Boil rapidly for a few minutes. Cool, then purée the celery.

4. Mash the blue cheese and mix to a smooth paste with the Ricotta cheese. Add the puréed celery and seasoning to taste.

5. Spoon the mixture into a bowl. Serve topped with soya (soy) 'bacon' bits.

PIQUANT AVOCADO PÂTÉ

Imperial (Metric)	**American**
½ small onion	½ small onion
½ green pepper	½ green pepper
1 large ripe avocado	1 large ripe avocado
6 oz (170g) low-fat soft cheese	¾ cup low-fat soft cheese
Seasoning to taste	Seasoning to taste
1 tablespoon lemon juice	1 tablespoon lemon juice
Fresh parsley	Fresh parsley
1 teaspoon *Holbrook's* Worcester Sauce, or to taste	1 teaspoon vegetarian Worcester Sauce, or to taste
10 stuffed olives, coarsely chopped	10 stuffed olives, coarsely chopped
1 oz (30g) walnuts to garnish	3 tablespoons English walnuts to garnish

1. Finely chop the onion and the pepper; peel and mash the avocado.

2. Blend together all the ingredients except the olives and walnuts.

3. When smooth and creamy, add the coarsely chopped olives. Spoon into a small dish. Chill the pâté well.

4. Serve sprinkled with walnut pieces.

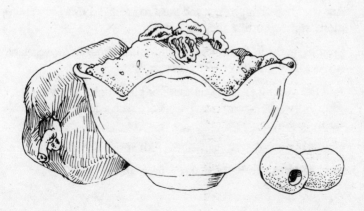

CHESTNUT PÂTÉ   OK

Imperial (Metric)	American
¾ lb (340g) chestnuts *	12 ounces chestnuts *
1 oz (30g) polyunsaturated margarine	2½ tablespoons polyunsaturated margarine
½ clove garlic, crushed	½ clove garlic, crushed
1 leek, finely chopped	1 leek, finely chopped
4 oz (115g) mushrooms, sliced	2 cups mushrooms, sliced
½ oz (15g) wholemeal flour	½ tablespoon wholewheat flour
⅛ pint (70ml) vegetable stock *or* water	¼ cup vegetable stock *or* water
Seasoning to taste	Seasoning to taste
Watercress to garnish	Watercress to garnish

(handwritten margin note: Don't to put too much w2.)

1. Slit the shells of the chestnuts, then drop them into a pan of boiling water. Cook for about 15 minutes, remove them from the water and cool slightly.

2. Use a sharp knife to peel away the outer shells and inner skins of the chestnuts. (This is easiest to do whilst they are still warm.) If the nuts are not yet tender, boil them a little longer in fresh water. Drain well and chop coarsely.

3. Meanwhile, melt the margarine in another saucepan and cook the garlic until it begins to soften.

4. Add the finely chopped leek and mushrooms and cook a few minutes more, stirring so that they do not burn.

5. Sprinkle in the flour, cook for 1 minute only. Pour in the vegetable stock, stir, and simmer to thicken.

6. Add the chestnuts and either mash or blend them to make a thick paste. Adjust the consistency, if necessary, with a little more vegetable stock. Season to taste.

7. Chill briefly and serve garnished with sprigs of watercress.

* Dried chestnuts can be used when fresh are not available.

'SAUSAGE' PÂTÉ

Imperial (Metric)	American
6 oz (170g) butter beans, soaked overnight	1 cup Lima beans, soaked overnight
1 oz (30g) wheatgerm	¼ cup wheatgerm
2 oz (55g) wholemeal breadcrumbs	½ cup wholewheat breadcrumbs
1 teaspoon marjoram	1 teaspoon marjoram
Seasoning to taste	Seasoning to taste
1 large egg, lightly beaten	1 large egg, lightly beaten
Parsley to garnish	Parsley to garnish

1. Put the beans in a saucepan with fresh water, and fast boil for 10 minutes. Cover the pan, lower heat, and simmer for 30-40 minutes or until well cooked.

2. Drain the beans and mash well.

3. Mix the bean purée with the wheatgerm, breadcrumbs, marjoram and seasoning.

4. Add the lightly beaten egg.

5. Transfer the mixture to a lightly greased pâté-type dish, smooth the top. Bake at 350°F/180°C (Gas Mark 4) for about 30 minutes, or until set. Put aside to cool.

6. Garnish with parsley and serve straight from the dish.

SUNFLOWER AND PEPPER PÂTÉ

Imperial (Metric)
5 oz (140g) sunflower seeds
1 red pepper
2 sticks celery
Approximately 4 tablespoons
  vegetable oil
Seasoning to taste
Celery leaves to garnish

American
1 cup sunflower seeds
1 red pepper
2 stalks celery
Approximately 4 tablespoons
  vegetable oil
Seasoning to taste
Celery leaves to garnish

1. Dry roast the seeds in a heavy pan (or in the oven) so that they are lightly and evenly browned.

2. Chop the pepper and celery.

3. Blend together the seeds, pepper and celery with just enough oil to make a smooth thick paste.

4. Season to taste, spoon into a small bowl, and chill.

5. Garnish with chopped celery leaves before serving.

POTTED MUSHROOMS WITH ALMONDS

Imperial (Metric)
1 oz (30g) polyunsaturated
  margarine
¾ lb (340g) chopped mushrooms
1 teaspoon chopped fresh marjoram
1 teaspoon chopped fresh parsley
Seasoning to taste
1 tablespoon white wine
2 oz (55g) ground almonds
1½ oz (45g) butter

American
2½ tablespoons polyunsaturated
  margarine
4½ cups chopped mushrooms
1 teaspoon chopped fresh marjoram
1 teaspoon chopped fresh parsley
Seasoning to taste
1 tablespoon white wine
½ cup ground almonds
3½ tablespoons butter

1. Melt the polyunsaturated margarine in a wide pan. Add the chopped mushrooms, herbs and seasoning. Pour in the wine.

2. Cook over a medium heat, stirring every now and again, until the mushrooms are soft and most of the liquid has evaporated.

3. Blend the mushrooms with any remaining juice to make a purée (or chop them as fine as possible with a knife).

4. Stir in the ground nuts. Pack the mixture into 4 ramekins, smooth the tops, and chill.

5. Melt the butter and pour some over the top of each of the ramekins. Chill again so that the butter sets hard.

SPINACH AND TOFU PÂTÉ

Imperial (Metric)	American
2 tablespoons vegetable oil	2 tablespoons vegetable oil
1 onion, sliced	1 onion, sliced
1 lb (455g) spinach	1 pound spinach
6 oz (170g) tofu	¾ cup tofu
1 tablespoon lemon juice	1 tablespoon lemon juice
½-1 teaspoon dried marjoram	½-1 teaspoon dried marjoram
Garlic salt	Garlic salt
Seasoning to taste	Seasoning to taste
Salted peanuts or soya 'bacon' bits to garnish	Salted peanuts or soy Bac-O-Bits to garnish

1. Heat the oil and fry the sliced onion until it begins to soften.

2. Add the washed, shredded spinach. Continue cooking until the spinach wilts.

3. Blend together the spinach mixture, tofu, lemon juice, marjoram and seasoning to make a thick creamy paste.

4. Turn the mixture into a serving dish and chill. Serve garnished with a few peanuts or soya (soy) 'bacon' bits.

CASHEW PÂTÉ

Imperial (Metric)	American
6 oz (170g) low-fat soft cheese	¾ cup low-fat soft cheese
4 oz (115g) cashew nuts	1 cup cashew nuts
1 tablespoon fresh parsley	1 tablespoon fresh parsley
1 tablespoon fresh chives	1 tablespoon fresh chives
Seasoning to taste	Seasoning to taste
2-3 tablespoons double cream	2-3 tablespoons heavy cream
Extra herbs and cashew nuts to garnish	Extra herbs and cashew nuts to garnish

1. Mash the cheese to soften.

2. Grind the raw nuts and mix them evenly into the cheese.

3. Chop the herbs, and add them to the other ingredients together with the seasoning.

4. Add enough cream to soften the mixture. Spoon into a serving dish, and chill well.

5. Serve garnished with fresh herbs and a sprinkling of cashew nut halves (roasted to add colour contrast).

CURD CHEESE AND 'BACON' PÂTÉ

Imperial (Metric)	American
½ lb (225g) curd cheese	1 cup curd cheese
1 tablespoon lemon juice	1 tablespoon lemon juice
1 tablespoon vegetable oil	1 tablespoon vegetable oil
½ small onion, finely chopped	½ small onion, finely chopped
1 tablespoon chopped parsley	1 tablespoon chopped parsley
2 oz (55g) soya 'bacon' bits	2 ounces soy *Bac-O-Bits*
Seasoning to taste	Seasoning to taste
Red pepper strips to garnish	Red pepper strips to garnish

1. Beat the cheese and lemon juice until the mixture is smooth.

2. Heat the oil and fry the finely chopped onion. When it begins to colour, add to the cheese.

3. Stir in the parsley, crumbled soya (soy) 'bacon' bits and seasoning, mixing well.

4. Transfer the pâté to a small serving dish and chill. Serve garnished with strips of red pepper arranged like the spokes of a wheel.

INDIAN EGG PÂTÉ

Imperial (Metric)	American
5 eggs	5 eggs
2 tablespoons vegetable oil	2 tablespoons vegetable oil
1 onion	1 onion
1/2-1 clove garlic, crushed	1/2-1 clove garlic, crushed
Pinch of turmeric	Pinch of turmeric
1/2-1 teaspoon curry powder	1/2-1 teaspoon curry powder
Seasoning to taste	Seasoning to taste
2-3 tablespoons natural yogurt	2-3 tablespoons plain yogurt
Mung bean sprouts to garnish	Mung bean sprouts to garnish

1. Boil the eggs for 10 minutes. Cool under the tap, remove shells, and mash the eggs with a fork to make a smooth paste. Set aside.

2. Heat the oil in a clean pan, and fry the finely chopped onion with the garlic until it begins to colour.

3. Add the spices and seasoning, and cook a few minutes more. Stir the egg mixture into the pan and mix thoroughly. Leave to cool.

4. Lighten the mixture by stirring in the yogurt, then transfer to a serving dish and smooth the top. Chill briefly. Sprinkle with beansprouts before serving.

PINEAPPLE HAZELNUT PÂTÉ

Imperial (Metric)
½ lb (225g) curd cheese
1 spring onion
½ small green pepper
4 oz (115g) pineapple*
4 oz (115g) roasted hazelnuts
Seasoning to taste

American
1 cup curd cheese
1 scallion
½ small green pepper
4 ounces pineapple*
1 cup roasted hazelnuts
Seasoning to taste

1. Mash the cheese until it is smooth.

2. Finely chop the onion (scallion) and pepper; crush the pineapple, coarsely chop the nuts.

3. Add the onion, pepper, pineapple, and most of the nuts to the cheese, mixing well. Season generously.

4. Transfer to a small bowl and chill well. Garnish with the remaining nuts.

*Use fresh pineapple, or the kind that is tinned in natural juice.

PUMPKIN PÂTÉ

Imperial (Metric)
1 lb (455g) pumpkin
2 tablespoons vegetable oil
½ onion, chopped
½ green pepper, chopped
2 eggs, lightly whisked
3 tablespoons cream
4 oz (115g) grated Cheddar cheese
2 oz (55g) wheatgerm
1 teaspoon mixed dried herbs
Seasoning to taste
Parsley to garnish

American
1 pound pumpkin
2 tablespoons vegetable oil
½ onion, chopped
½ green pepper, chopped
2 eggs, lightly whisked
3 tablespoons cream
1 cup grated Cheddar cheese
½ cup wheatgerm
1 teaspoon mixed dried herbs
Seasoning to taste
Parsley to garnish

1. Peel the pumpkin, cube the flesh, and steam for 15 minutes, or until tender. Drain well, and cool.

2. Heat the oil in a clean pan, and fry the chopped onion and pepper to soften.

3. Mix together the puréed pumpkin, vegetables, lightly whisked eggs and cream. Add the grated cheese, wheatgerm, herbs and seasoning.

4. Spoon the mixture into a small, well-greased loaf tin. (If liked you can line it first with silver foil.) Stand in a tray containing at least 1 inch (2.5cm) of hot water.

5. Bake at 350°F/180°C (Gas Mark 4) for about an hour, or until set. Cool, then chill briefly.

6. Tip the pâté very carefully onto a flat plate, and garnish with parsley. Serve cut into slices.

TAHINI PARSLEY PÂTÉ

Imperial (Metric)	American
¼ pint (140ml) tahini	⅔ cup tahini
⅛ pint (70ml) hot vegetable stock	¼ cup hot vegetable stock
3 tablespoons parsley	3 tablespoons parsley
2 tablespoons lemon juice	2 tablespoons lemon juice
1 teaspoon made up mustard	1 teaspoon made up mustard
Seasoning to taste	Seasoning to taste
Approximately 2 oz (55g) wholemeal breadcrumbs	Approximately 1 cup wholewheat breadcrumbs
1 tomato to garnish	1 tomato to garnish

1. Stir the tahini into the vegetable stock.

2. Add the parsley, lemon juice, mustard and seasoning.

3. Stir in enough breadcrumbs to thicken the mixture. Spoon it into a small dish, smooth the top, and chill briefly.

4. Garnish with slices of tomato and maybe some extra sprigs of parsley before serving.

CURRIED VEGETABLE PÂTÉ

Imperial (Metric)	American
3 tablespoons vegetable oil	3 tablespoons vegetable oil
1 clove garlic, crushed	1 clove garlic, crushed
1 onion	1 onion
1 teaspoon cumin	1 teaspoon cumin
1 teaspoon coriander	1 teaspoon coriander
½ teaspoon turmeric	½ teaspoon turmeric
4 oz (115g) mushrooms	2 cups mushrooms
1 courgette	1 zucchini
¼ small cauliflower	¼ small cauliflower
4 oz (115g) peas, cooked	⅔ cup peas, cooked
2 oz (55g) creamed coconut	¼ cup creamed coconut
Cucumber slices to garnish	Cucumber slices to garnish

1. Heat the oil in a large pan. Add the garlic and chopped onion, and cook gently for 5-10 minutes to soften.

2. Add the spices, stir, and cook a few minutes more.

3. Clean and chop the mushrooms and the courgette (zucchini). Break the cauliflower into small florets. Mix the vegetables into the spices, add the peas, plus just a little cold water.

4. Cook gently until the vegetables are tender. Then raise the heat and cook, uncovered, to thicken any remaining liquid.

5. Grate the coconut and stir it into other ingredients so that it dissolves.

6. Mash or blend the vegetables and sauce to make a thick purée. Turn into a serving dish and chill well. Serve garnished with cucumber slices.

POTTED CHEESE

Imperial (Metric)	American
3 oz (85g) butter	1/3 cup butter
1/2 lb (225g) Caerphilly cheese	2 cups Caerphilly cheese
3 tablespoons soured cream	3 tablespoons soured cream
Fresh chopped mint	Fresh chopped mint
Seasoning to taste	Seasoning to taste
1/2 oz (15g) walnuts to garnish	1 1/2 tablespoons English walnuts to garnish

1. Mash the butter until soft and creamy.

2. Coarsely grate or crumble the cheese, and then mash together with the butter until completely smooth.

3. Add the soured cream, a generous amount of fresh chopped mint, and seasoning to taste.

4. Transfer to a dish or earthenware pot. Press down firmly, cover, and chill well.

5. Stand the cheese at room temperature for a short time before serving sprinkled with chopped walnuts.

OLIVE PÂTÉ

Imperial (Metric)	American
4 oz (115g) green olives*	1 cup green olives*
1 tablespoon lemon juice	1 tablespoon lemon juice
1 tablespoon vegetable oil	1 tablespoon vegetable oil
Seasoning to taste	Seasoning to taste
Approximately 1 oz (30g) wholemeal breadcrumbs	Approximately ½ cup wholewheat breadcrumbs
Parsley and spring onions to garnish	Parsley and scallions to garnish

1. Remove the stones from the olives.

2. Put the olives into a blender with the lemon juice, vegetable oil, seasoning to taste (you may not need salt as the olives will probably be salty enough). Blend until smooth.

3. Stir in breadcrumbs to thicken the pâté. Spoon into a small dish, and smooth the top.

4. Garnish with chopped parsley and spring onions (scallions), and serve at room temperature.

*Try this with black olives for a change. It is also interesting made with green stuffed olives.

AUTUMN PÂTÉ

Imperial (Metric)
1 small potato
1 small carrot
1 small parsnip
1 small leek
1 oz (30g) bulgur
2 oz (55g) aduki beans, cooked*
½ teaspoon basil
½ teaspoon rosemary, crumbled
Seasoning to taste
1 tablespoon tomato purée
1-2 tablespoons vegetable oil
Watercress to garnish

American
1 small potato
1 small carrot
1 small parsnip
1 small leek
1½ tablespoons bulgur
¼ cup aduki beans, cooked*
½ teaspoon basil
½ teaspoon rosemary, crumbled
Seasoning to taste
1 tablespoon tomato paste
1-2 tablespoons vegetable oil
Watercress to garnish

1. Peel and cube the potato, carrot and parsnip. Clean and chop the leek. Steam or boil the vegetables until tender.

2. Soak the bulgur in boiling water (you can use the stock from the vegetables for this). Cover and leave for 30 minutes.

3. In a blender combine the vegetables, bulgur, aduki beans, herbs and seasoning. When smooth, stir in the tomato purée (paste) and enough vegetable oil to give a smooth texture.

4. Transfer the pâté to a small dish, smooth the top. Cover and chill before serving garnished with the watercress.

*Although the beans can be cooked specially for this pâté, it's an ideal opportunity to use up left-overs.

'PORK' AND PEPPER TERRINE

Imperial (Metric)	American
5 oz (140g) soya 'pork' chunks	5 ounces soy 'pork' chunks
1 tablespoon vegetable oil	1 tablespoon vegetable oil
2 egg whites (large)	2 egg whites (large)
6 oz (170g) Ricotta cheese	¾ cup Ricotta cheese
Seasoning to taste	Seasoning to taste
Good pinch of paprika	Good pinch of paprika
2-3 tablespoons vegetable oil	2-3 tablespoons vegetable oil
1 large red pepper, coarsely chopped	1 large red pepper, coarsely chopped
1 large green pepper, coarsely chopped	1 large green pepper, coarsely chopped

1. Put the soya (soy) 'pork' chunks into a saucepan, cover with cold water, add 1 tablespoon of oil. Bring gently to a boil, then simmer (follow instructions on pack for cooking time).

2. Drain the 'pork' then chop finely, or mince.

3. Whisk the egg whites lightly, soften the Ricotta cheese, then mix both with the chopped 'pork'. Add seasoning and paprika.

4. In a clean pan heat the vegetable oil and gently fry the coarsely chopped peppers until they are soft. Drain on paper towels.

5. Line an earthenware terrine or loaf tin with greased aluminium foil.

6. Spoon about a third of the 'pork' mixture across the bottom, top with half of the peppers. Repeat this once more, then finish with a final layer of 'pork'.

7. Cover with a lid or more foil, and stand the terrine or tin in a bain-marie, or another pan containing at least 1 inch (2.5cm) of boiling water.

8. Bake at 425°F/220°C (Gas Mark 7) for about 40 minutes, or until set. Leave to cool to room temperature, then chill. Turn out carefully onto a plate just before serving.

LENTIL, NUT AND MUSHROOM TERRINE

Imperial (Metric)	American
1 tablespoon vegetable oil	1 tablespoon vegetable oil
1 clove garlic, crushed	1 clove garlic, crushed
2 spring onions, chopped	2 scallions, chopped
1 stick celery, chopped	1 stalk celery, chopped
Small tin of tomatoes	Small can of tomatoes
5 oz (140g) split red lentils	¾ cup split red lentils
5 oz (140g) mixed nuts, ground	1¼ cups mixed nuts, ground
2 small eggs	2 small eggs
Seasoning to taste	Seasoning to taste
1 tablespoon chopped parsley	1 tablespoon chopped parsley
4 oz (115g) button mushrooms	2 cups button mushrooms
Parsley to garnish	Parsley to garnish

1. Heat the oil in a large pan. Gently fry the crushed garlic, chopped onions and celery to soften.

2. Add the contents of the tin of tomatoes, breaking them up. Cook until the sauce is thick.

3. Meanwhile, cook the lentils in boiling water (or vegetable stock) for 15-20 minutes. Drain well.

4. Stir together the tomato sauce, lentils, and ground nuts. Allow the mixture to cool. Beat the eggs and add them to the other ingredients, seasoning well. Add the parsley.

5. Line an earthenware terrine or loaf tin with greased aluminium foil.

6. Spoon in half of the lentil and nut mixture, smoothing the top.

7. Arrange the cleaned mushrooms neatly over the first mixture. These can be left whole, or halved.

8. Finish with the rest of the lentil and nut mixture. Cover with a lid or foil, and stand the container in a bain-marie, or a large tin holding at least 1 inch (2.5cm) of boiling water.

9. Bake at 400°F/200°C (Gas Mark 6) for 1 hour, or until set. Leave to cool in the terrine. Chill before serving garnished with parsley.

MIXED VEGETABLE TERRINE

Imperial (Metric)	American
Approximately 2 oz (55g) butter *or* polyunsaturated margarine	¼ cup butter *or* polyunsaturated margarine
1 lb (455g) carrots, sliced	1 pound carrots, sliced
6 oz (170g) peas, fresh or frozen	1 cup peas, fresh or frozen
1 onion, sliced	1 onion, sliced
1 lb (455g) spinach	1 pound spinach
4 eggs	4 eggs
4 oz (115g) grated Gruyère cheese	1 cup grated Gruyère cheese
Seasoning to taste	Seasoning to taste
Good pinch of nutmeg	Good pinch of nutmeg

1. Melt half the fat in a heavy based saucepan. Add the sliced carrots and cook for a few minutes, stirring occasionally. Cover the pan and simmer the carrots for 10 minutes more, checking that they do not burn. Add a little more fat if necessary. Chop coarsely and set aside.

2. Cook the peas in water until tender. Drain well and mix with the carrots.

3. In a clean pan melt the rest of the fat. Add the sliced onion and cook until it begins to soften.

4. Add the washed, shredded spinach (shake off excess water, and do not add more). Cook gently, stirring now and again, until wilted, then chop finely.

5. Beat three of the eggs; add the grated cheese, seasoning and nutmeg.

6. Stir the carrots and peas into this mixture.

7. Beat the remaining egg and add to the spinach.

8. Use an earthenware terrine, or a loaf tin. Line with greased aluminium foil.

9. Spread half of the carrot mixture across the bottom, top with the spinach, finish with the remaining carrot. Smooth the top.

10. Cover tightly with a lid or more aluminium foil, and stand the terrine or tin in a bain-marie (or another pan containing at least 1 inch [2.5cm] of very hot water).

11. Bake at 400°F/200°C (Gas Mark 6) for about an hour, or until a knife inserted in the centre comes out clean.

12. Remove from the oven and let it stand for at least 10 minutes before taking out of the terrine very carefully, if you intend to serve it warm. If you prefer a cold dish, do not remove it from the terrine but chill as it is. Serve cut into slices.

3.
COLD DIPS

GUACAMOLE

Imperial (Metric)
1 large ripe avocado
1 large tomato, finely chopped
½ small onion, finely chopped
1 clove garlic, finely crushed
1 tablespoon lemon juice
Seasoning to taste
⅓ pint (200ml) soured cream

American
1 large ripe avocado
1 large tomato, finely chopped
½ small onion, finely chopped
1 clove garlic, finely crushed
1 tablespoon lemon juice
Seasoning to taste
¾ cup soured cream

1. Peel, stone and mash the avocado.

2. Stir in the chopped tomato, onion and garlic.

3. Add lemon juice, seasoning, and then the soured cream, mixing all the ingredients together thoroughly.

4. Turn into a serving dish and chill before serving.

TOFU AVOCADO DIP

Imperial (Metric)	American
2 medium ripe avocados	2 medium ripe avocados
2 tablespoons lemon juice	2 tablespoons lemon juice
½ lb (225g) tofu	1 cup tofu
7 oz (200g) tin tomatoes	7 ounce can tomatoes
½ small onion, chopped	½ small onion, chopped
1 teaspoon chilli powder, or to taste	1 teaspoon chili powder, or to taste
Seasoning to taste	Seasoning to taste
1-2 tablespoons mayonnaise	1-2 tablespoons mayonnaise

1. Peel, then mash the avocados together with the lemon juice.

2. Drain and crumble the tofu. Drain the tomatoes.

3. In a blender, mix together the avocados, tofu, tomatoes, onion, chilli powder and seasoning.

4. Stir in just enough mayonnaise to give the mixture a dip consistency.

5. Turn into a serving dish (or pack back into the avocado skins). Chill briefly before serving.

WALNUT DIP

Imperial (Metric)	American
5 oz (140g) walnuts	1 cup English walnuts
2 tablespoons chopped parsley	2 tablespoons chopped parsley
¼ pint (140ml) double cream	⅔ cup heavy cream
Seasoning to taste	Seasoning to taste
Extra parsley to garnish	Extra parsley to garnish

1. Grind the nuts coarsely.

2. Mix the nuts and parsley with the cream, making sure they are evenly distributed.

3. Season well to taste. Transfer to a small dish.

4. Chill briefly before serving topped with parsley sprigs.

BLUE CHEESE DIP

Imperial (Metric)	American
4 oz (115g) Gorgonzola or other blue cheese	1 cup Gorgonzola or other blue cheese
¼ pint (140ml) natural yogurt	⅔ cup plain yogurt
½ ripe avocado, mashed	½ ripe avocado, mashed
2 tablespoons finely chopped chives	2 tablespoons finely chopped chives
1 oz (30g) salted pistachio nuts, finely chopped	3 tablespoons salted pistachio nuts, finely chopped

1. Break the cheese into small pieces.

2. Mash the cheese then stir in the yogurt, mashed avocado and chives, and mix until smooth (or use a blender).

3. Season to taste. Chill until required. Top with the finely chopped pistachio nuts.

HUMMUS WITH YOGURT

Imperial (Metric)	American
½ lb (225g) chick peas, soaked overnight	1 cup garbanzo beans, soaked overnight
2 cloves garlic, crushed	2 cloves garlic, crushed
3 tablespoons tahini	3 tablespoons tahini
2 tablespoons vegetable oil	2 tablespoons vegetable oil
2 tablespoons lemon juice	2 tablespoons lemon juice
Approximately 3 tablespoons natural yogurt	Approximately 3 tablespoons plain yogurt
Seasoning to taste	Seasoning to taste
¼ teaspoon ground cumin	¼ teaspoon ground cumin
Parsley to garnish	Parsley to garnish

1. Put the chick peas (garbanzos) into a saucepan, cover with fresh water, and bring to a boil. Continue boiling for 10 minutes, then lower the heat and simmer for 1-1½ hours, or until tender. Drain well.

2. In a blender combine the chick peas (garbanzos), garlic, tahini, vegetable oil and lemon juice to make a thick, smooth paste. Alternatively, you could grind the chick peas (garbanzos) to a powder, then combine with the other ingredients.

3. Mix in enough yogurt to soften the paste so that it is the consistency of a dip. Season well, add cumin, and transfer to a small dish.

4. Chill the hummus, then serve it garnished with chopped parsley.

SPINACH DIP

Imperial (Metric)	American
½ lb (225g) spinach	8 ounces spinach
2 oz (55g) walnuts	½ cup English walnuts
1 clove garlic, crushed	1 clove garlic, crushed
4 tablespoons vegetable oil	4 tablespoons vegetable oil
Seasoning to taste	Seasoning to taste
Good pinch of raw cane sugar	Good pinch of raw cane sugar
Good pinch of ground nutmeg	Good pinch of ground nutmeg
Approximately ¼ pint (140ml) natural yogurt	⅔ cup plain yogurt

1. Wash, shred and steam the spinach for literally a minute or two to soften. Cool and drain well, reserving the water.

2. In a blender combine the walnuts, garlic and a drop of the spinach water.

3. When well mixed, add the oil and spinach, alternating them, until the mixture is smooth and fairly thick.

4. Add seasoning, sugar and nutmeg. Stir in the yogurt to make a dipping consistency.

COTTAGE CHEESE DIP WITH CARAWAY

Imperial (Metric)	American
½ lb (225g) cottage cheese	1 cup cottage cheese
½ small onion, finely chopped	½ small onion, finely chopped
1 tablespoon capers	1 tablespoon capers
Pinch of dry mustard	Pinch of dry mustard
Seasoning to taste	Seasoning to taste
Approximately ½ oz (15g) caraway seeds	1½ tablespoons caraway seeds
Paprika to garnish	Paprika to garnish

1. Beat, sieve or blend the cottage cheese until smooth.

2. Add the finely chopped onion and capers.

3. Stir in the mustard and seasoning to taste. Crush the caraway seeds coarsely and add to the other ingredients.

4. Transfer the mixture to a small bowl, cover, and chill well before serving. Sprinkle with paprika before serving.

TAHINI AND TOFU DIP

Imperial (Metric)	**American**
½ lb (225g) tofu	1 cup tofu
4 tablespoons tahini	4 tablespoons tahini
2 tablespoons vegetable oil	2 tablespoons vegetable oil
Good squeeze of lemon juice	Good squeeze of lemon juice
Garlic salt	Garlic salt
Seasoning to taste	Seasoning to taste
Parsley, chopped	Parsley, chopped

1. Drain the tofu, then purée in a blender or mash by hand.

2. Stir in the tahini, vegetable oil and lemon juice, mixing well. If the mixture seems too thick, add a drop more lemon juice or water.

3. Flavour well with the garlic salt, seasoning and chopped parsley.

4. Serve topped with extra parsley, if liked.

CREAMY MOUSSE DIP

Imperial (Metric)	**American**
1 large egg white	1 large egg white
¼ pint (140ml) soured cream	⅔ cup soured cream
¼ pint (140ml) mayonnaise	⅔ cup mayonnaise
Sea or rock salt	Sea or rock salt
½-1 teaspoon paprika	½-1 teaspoon paprika
Roasted hazelnuts, coarsely chopped, to garnish	Roasted hazelnuts, coarsely chopped, to garnish

1. Whisk the egg white until stiff enough to hold a shape.

2. Fold in the soured cream and mayonnaise as gently as possible, together with a little salt and the paprika.

3. Transfer the mixture to a small bowl, and serve at once garnished with coarsely chopped roasted hazelnuts.

SWEETCORN DIP

Imperial (Metric)
4 oz (115g) sweetcorn
½ lb (225g) Cheddar cheese
¼ pint (140ml) whipping cream
½ small green pepper
½ small onion
Seasoning to taste

American
⅔ cup sweetcorn
2 cups Cheddar cheese
⅔ cup whipping cream
½ small green pepper
½ small onion
Seasoning to taste

1. Cook the sweetcorn in boiling water until tender. Drain well, and set aside to cool.

2. Grate the cheese.

3. Very lightly whip the cream until it begins to thicken. Stir in the sweetcorn and cheese, mixing well.

4. Chop the pepper and onion, and add these to the other ingredients. Season to taste. Serve at once.

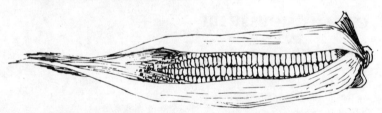

LANCASHIRE DIP WITH MUSHROOMS

Imperial (Metric)
½ lb (225g) Lancashire cheese
1 oz (30g) polyunsaturated
    margarine
3 oz (85g) mushrooms, chopped
1 stick celery, finely chopped
¼ pint (140ml) single cream
Seasoning to taste
Approximately ½ teaspoon caraway
    seeds
Watercress to garnish

American
2 cups Lancashire cheese
2½ tablespoons polyunsaturated
    margarine
1 cup mushrooms, chopped
1 stalk celery, finely chopped
⅔ cup light cream
Seasoning to taste
Approximately ½ teaspoon caraway
    seeds
Watercress to garnish

1.   Grate the cheese as fine as possible.

2.   Melt the margarine in a saucepan and add the chopped mushrooms.
     Cook for a just a few minutes to soften.

3.   Add the finely chopped celery and cook a minute more.

4.   Stir together the cheese, vegetables and cream, mixing them
     thoroughly. (Adjust the consistency, if necessary, with more cream,
     milk or water).

5.   Flavour with seasoning and caraway seeds.

6.   Serve garnished with sprigs of watercress.

AUBERGINE YOGURT DIP   ± some red wine vinegar

Imperial (Metric)
2 medium aubergines
1 tablespoon olive oil
1 tablespoon lemon juice
1 clove garlic, chopped or crushed
1 medium green pepper
Seasoning to taste
¼ pint (140ml) natural yogurt
Black olives to garnish

American
2 medium eggplants
1 tablespoon olive oil
1 tablespoon lemon juice
1 clove garlic, chopped or crushed
1 medium green pepper
Seasoning to taste
⅔ cup plain yogurt
Black olives to garnish

1.   Pierce the skin of the aubergines (eggplants) with a fork. Bake on
     a tray at 400°F/200°C (Gas Mark 6) for 45 minutes, or until very soft.

2.   Cool the aubergines (eggplants), cut in half, and scoop out the flesh.

3.   In a bowl mash together the flesh with the olive oil, lemon juice,
     very finely chopped or crushed garlic and pepper.

4.   When well blended, stir in seasoning and the yogurt.

5.   Chill in a covered dish before serving. Garnish with a ring of black
     olives.

AUBERGINE DIP WITH TAHINI

Imperial (Metric)	American
1 large aubergine	1 large eggplant
Approximately 4 tablespoons tahini	Approximately 4 tablespoons tahini
1 tablespoon lemon juice	1 tablespoon lemon juice
1 tablespoon vegetable oil	1 tablespoon vegetable oil
4 tablespoons chopped parsley	4 tablespoons chopped parsley
Seasoning to taste	Seasoning to taste
1 tomato to garnish	1 tomato to garnish

1. Pierce the skin of the aubergine (eggplant), and bake in the oven at 400°F/200°C (Gas Mark 6) for 50-60 minutes, or until the skin is black, the inner flesh very soft.

2. When cool enough to handle, cut the aubergine (eggplant) in half, scoop out the flesh and mash well in a bowl.

3. Add the tahini, lemon juice, vegetable oil, parsley and seasoning, and mix thoroughly to make a smooth purée. (This can be done in a blender for a smoother dip). If necessary, thin the mixture with a drop of water, lemon juice or oil.

4. Spoon into a serving bowl and chill before serving. Tomato slices make an attractive garnish.

CHEESY PINEAPPLE DIP

Imperial (Metric)	American
¾ lb (340g) low-fat soft cheese	1½ cups low-fat soft cheese
7-oz (200g) tin pineapple pieces in natural juice	7-ounce can pineapple pieces in natural juice
¼ small melon	¼ small melon
1 celery stick	1 celery stalk
2 oz (55g) almond flakes	½ cup slivered almonds

1. Mash the cheese to soften.

2. Chop up the pineapple, and stir it into the cheese together with enough of the juice to make a dip consistency.

3. Chop the melon and add to the other ingredients.

4. Chop the celery and add to the cheese mixture. Transfer the dip to a serving dish.

5. In a dry pan roast the flaked nuts until lightly coloured. Cool, then sprinkle them over the dip. Serve at once.

CURRIED TOFU DIP

Imperial (Metric)	American
½ lb (225g) tofu	1 cup tofu
2 tablespoons lemon juice	2 tablespoons lemon juice
2 tablespoons vegetable oil	2 tablespoons vegetable oil
3 spring onions	3 scallions
Approximately ½ teaspoon curry powder	Approximately ½ teaspoon curry powder
Seasoning to taste	Seasoning to taste
Chopped cucumber to garnish	Chopped cucumber to garnish

1. Drain the tofu well, then purée in a blender or mash by hand.

2. Add the lemon juice, vegetable oil and finely chopped spring onions (scallions). Flavour to taste with curry powder and seasoning.

3. Chill briefly to allow the flavours to develop. Adjust the seasoning before serving, and if the dip is too thick, add more liquid — lemon juice, oil, or a drop of water. Mix well.

4. Sprinkle with finely chopped cucumber.

COCONUT DIP

Imperial (Metric)
½ lb (225g) Quark cheese
4 oz (115g) desiccated coconut
2-4 tablespoons single cream or top
  of the milk
1 teaspoon honey, or to taste

American
1 cup Quark cheese
1⅓ cups desiccated coconut
2-4 tablespoons light cream or half
  and half
1 teaspoon honey, or to taste

1. Sieve the Quark cheese until it is smooth and creamy.

2. Stir in the coconut, and enough cream to make a smooth dipping consistency.

3. If liked, this dip can be slightly sweetened with honey. Chill briefly before serving.

Note: Although fruit goes well with this unusual dip, try it too with celery and carrot sticks.

LENTIL DIP

Imperial (Metric)	American
5 oz (140g) split red lentils	¾ cup split red lentils
2 tablespoons vegetable oil	2 tablespoons vegetable oil
1 small onion	1 small onion
1 small clove garlic, crushed	1 small clove garlic, crushed
Soya sauce	Soy sauce
Good pinch of ground ginger	Good pinch of ground ginger
Good squeeze of lemon juice	Good squeeze of lemon juice
Chopped parsley	Chopped parsley
Seasoning to taste	Seasoning to taste
Twist of lemon to garnish	Twist of lemon to garnish

1. Put the lentils into a saucepan with enough cold water to cover. Bring to the boil, then cover pan and simmer the lentils for about 20 minutes, or until soft enough to make a purée. Check the water every now and again.

2. Heat the oil in a clean saucepan. Add the chopped onion and garlic, and cook until soft.

3. Drain the lentils, reserving the liquid. Mash them, then add to the onion and garlic together with the soya (soy) sauce, ginger, lemon juice, a generous amount of chopped parsley, and seasoning to taste.

4. Pour in enough of the liquid in which the lentils were cooked, to make a dipping consistency. The dip can be served as it is, or processed to make it smoother. Adjust seasoning.

5. Chill, and serve garnished with a twist of lemon.

GARLIC MAYONNAISE WITH PINE NUTS

Imperial (Metric)	American
1 egg (at room temperature)	1 egg (at room temperature)
Good pinch of dry mustard	Good pinch of dry mustard
Seasoning to taste	Seasoning to taste
¼ pint (140ml) olive oil	⅔ cup olive oil
¼ pint (140ml) vegetable oil	⅔ cup vegetable oil
1 tablespoon white wine vinegar	1 tablespoon white wine vinegar
1-2 cloves garlic, crushed	1-2 cloves garlic, crushed
¼ oz (7g) polyunsaturated margarine	½ tablespoon polyunsaturated margarine
1 oz (30g) pine nuts	3 tablespoons pine nuts

1. Break the egg into a blender, add the mustard and seasoning.

2. Blend gradually, adding the oil a little at a time. When the mixture begins to thicken the remaining oil can be added more quickly.

3. Mix in the wine vinegar and crushed garlic, and process until smooth and creamy.

4. Adjust the seasoning if necessary. Chill before serving (mayonnaise keeps for up to a week if stored in a fridge).

5. Meanwhile, melt the fat and fry the pine nuts until light brown in colour. Drain well and cool. Sprinkle over the mayonnaise, or stir most of them into it, reserving just a few for a garnish.

Note: This rich mayonnaise, when used as a dip, goes especially well with crudités (strips or small pieces of raw vegetables).

GREEN MAYONNAISE

Imperial (Metric)	American
²/₃ pint (340ml) mayonnaise	1¹/₂ cups mayonnaise
1 tablespoon lemon juice	1 tablespoon lemon juice
¹/₂ small onion, chopped	¹/₂ small onion, chopped
2 tablespoons chopped parsley	2 tablespoons chopped parsley
2 tablespoons chopped watercress	2 tablespoons chopped watercress
1 teaspoon capers	1 teaspoon capers
Seasoning — optional	Seasoning — optional

1. Put all the ingredients into a blender and whizz until smooth. Add seasoning if necessary, though the mayonnaise will already have a good flavour.

2. Serve at once, or keep in the fridge until needed.

SKORDALIA

Imperial (Metric)	American
3 cloves garlic	3 cloves garlic
Seasoning to taste	Seasoning to taste
1 egg yolk	1 egg yolk
1 tablespoon lemon juice	1 tablespoon lemon juice
Approximately ¼ pint (140ml) olive oil	⅔ cup olive oil
2oz (55g) ground almonds, preferably fresh ground	½ cup ground almonds, preferably fresh ground
Roasted sesame seeds and parsley to garnish	Roasted sesame seeds and parsley to garnish

1. Grind the garlic cloves in a mortar and pestle (or grinder) to make a smooth paste.

2. Add the seasoning, egg yolk and lemon juice, mixing well.

3. Gradually add the olive oil, drop by drop, so that it is completely absorbed.

4. Stir in the almonds, mixing briskly to make a smooth paste.

5. Serve topped with seeds and sprigs of parsley.

Note: To make this dip into a pâté, stir in 2-3oz (55-85g) fine wholemeal breadcrumbs.

GRIBICHE DIP

Imperial (Metric)
3 hard-boiled eggs
1 tablespoon made-up mustard
1 tablespoon chopped fresh
  tarragon*
1/3 pint (200ml) vegetable oil
  (preferably olive)
1 teaspoon white wine vinegar
Seasoning to taste
Watercress to garnish

American
3 hard-boiled eggs
1 tablespoon made-up mustard
1 tablespoon chopped fresh
  tarragon*
3/4 cup vegetable oil (preferably olive)
1 teaspoon white wine vinegar
Seasoning to taste
Watercress to garnish

1. Carefully halve the eggs, remove the yolks and mash them together.

2. Mix the yolks with the mustard and tarragon.

3. Gradually add the oil drop by drop, stirring continually. Stir in the wine vinegar. Season to taste.

4. Chop the egg whites as fine as possible and mix into the sauce. Chill briefly.

5. Stir the dip well before serving garnished with sprigs of watercress.

*If tarragon is unavailable, use any other fresh herb, alone or in a combination. Dried herbs are nowhere near as good in this particular recipe.

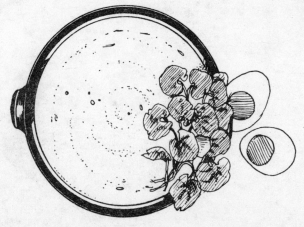

VEGETABLE DIP

Imperial (Metric)	American
1 medium onion	1 medium onion
2 medium carrots	2 medium carrots
2 large tomatoes	2 large tomatoes
2 sticks celery	2 stalks celery
Approximately ¼ pint (140ml) vegetable stock	⅔ cup vegetable stock
Squeeze of lemon juice	Squeeze of lemon juice
1-2 teaspoons mixed dried herbs	1-2 teaspoons mixed dried herbs
Seasoning to taste	Seasoning to taste
1-2 tablespoons tahini, cream *or* yogurt	1-2 tablespoons tahini, cream *or* yogurt
Parsley to garnish	Parsley to garnish

1. Peel the onion and carrots. Chop all the vegetables into small pieces.

2. Put them into a saucepan with the stock, lemon juice, herbs and seasoning, and cook until tender. Top up the liquid if necessary.

3. Cool the vegetables slightly, drain well and reserve the liquid, then purée them in a blender. Adjust the seasoning.

4. Add tahini, cream or yogurt, mixing well. If necessary, add a little of the liquid in which the vegetables were cooked, to make the dip the right consistency.

5. Serve warm or cold, garnished with parsley.

CHILLI PEANUT DIP

Imperial (Metric)	**American**
4 oz (115g) peanut butter	½ cup peanut butter
⅓ pint (200ml) vegetable stock	¾ cup vegetable stock
1 finely grated carrot	1 finely grated carrot
Soya sauce	Soy sauce
A squeeze of lemon juice	A squeeze of lemon juice
1 teaspoon honey	1 teaspoon honey
½ teaspoon chilli powder or to taste	½ teaspoon chili powder or to taste
Vegetable oil (optional)	Vegetable oil (optional)

1. Put the peanut butter into a bowl.

2. Pour on the warmed vegetable stock and stir well until all the liquid has been absorbed.

3. Stir in the grated carrot.

4. Add the soya (soy) sauce, lemon juice, honey and chilli powder, adjusting the quantities to get the taste you prefer.

5. If necessary, add a little more stock, or a few tablespoons of vegetable oil to thin the dip.

6. Serve at once. Celery sticks are delicious with this dip.

FETA CHEESE DIP

Imperial (Metric)
4 oz (115g) Feta cheese
2 spring onions
½ clove garlic
2 tablespoons vegetable oil
1 tablespoon lemon juice
1 tablespoon chopped coriander
  leaves
Creamy milk to mix
Toasted almond flakes to garnish

American
½ cup Feta cheese
2 scallions
½ clove garlic
2 tablespoons vegetable oil
1 tablespoon lemon juice
1 tablespoon chopped cilantro leaves
Creamy milk to mix
Toasted almond flakes to garnish

1. Crumble the cheese into a bowl.

2. Finely chop the spring onions (scallions) and garlic.

3. Combine the cheese, onions and garlic, vegetable oil, lemon juice and coriander (cilantro) leaves. Mash together.

4. Add enough milk to give the mixture a dipping consistency. There should be plenty of flavour in this dip, but if necessary, add seasoning.

5. Turn into a dish, and chill briefly before serving sprinkled with the toasted almond flakes.

SWEET AND SOUR DIP WITH OLIVES

Imperial (Metric)
⅓ pint (200ml) soured cream
1 tablespoon lemon juice
¼ oz (7g) raw cane sugar*,
   powdered in grinder
Seasoning to taste
12 black olives

American
¾ cup soured cream
1 tablespoon lemon juice
½ tablespoon raw cane sugar*,
   powdered in grinder
Seasoning to taste
12 black olives

1. Mix together the soured cream and lemon juice.

2. Stir in the sugar, making sure it is thoroughly blended. Season to taste.

3. Remove the stones from the olives and chop the flesh as fine as possible. Stir into the other ingredients. Chill before serving.

*Use the very palest sugar for this recipe — darker sugars, though more nutritious, will spoil the colour.

4.

HOT DIPS

HOT CHEESE DIP

Imperial (Metric)
2 tablespoons vegetable oil
1 small onion, finely chopped
1 clove garlic, crushed
14-oz (395g) tin tomatoes
½ lb (225g) Cheddar cheese, grated
¼ pint (140ml) single cream
Pinch of chilli powder, to taste
Seasoning to taste
Parsley to garnish

American
2 tablespoons vegetable oil
1 small onion, finely chopped
1 clove garlic, crushed
14-ounce can tomatoes
2 cups Cheddar cheese, grated
⅔ cup light cream
Pinch of chili powder, to taste
Seasoning to taste
Parsley to garnish

1. Heat the vegetable oil in a saucepan and fry the finely chopped onion and garlic until they begin to soften.

2. Drain the tomatoes, saving the juice for use in another recipe. Crush the tomatoes and add to the saucepan. Bring to the boil, then cook gently for 3-5 minutes.

3. Add the grated cheese and leave over a low heat, stirring continually, until melted.

4. Remove the saucepan from the cooker and add the cream, chilli powder and seasoning. Turn into a warmed dish and serve at once topped with freshly chopped parsley.

BARBECUE DIP

Imperial (Metric)
1 oz (30g) polyunsaturated
  margarine
1 onion
1 clove garlic, crushed
1 lb (455g) tomatoes, or tinned
  equivalent
1 teaspoon thyme
Approximately ¼ pint (140ml) white
  wine
Seasoning to taste

American
2½ tablespoons polyunsaturated
  margarine
1 onion
1 clove garlic, crushed
1 pound tomatoes, or canned
  equivalent
1 teaspoon thyme
⅔ cup white wine
Seasoning to taste

1. Melt the margarine and fry the finely chopped onion and the garlic until beginning to soften.

2. Add the peeled chopped tomatoes, thyme and wine. Bring to a boil, then lower the heat and simmer the ingredients to make a purée.

3. Adjust the consistency, if necessary, with a drop more wine or water. Season well to taste. Pour at once into a warmed dish and serve.

Note: This dip is especially tasty with deep fried mushrooms or other vegetables.

YOGURT HOLLANDAISE DIP

Imperial (Metric)
2 large eggs
½ pint (285ml) natural yogurt
Good pinch of cayenne pepper
Seasoning to taste
Soya 'bacon' bits to garnish
  optional

American
2 large eggs
1⅓ cups plain yogurt
Good pinch of cayenne pepper
Seasoning to taste
Soy *Bac-O-Bits* to garnish (optional)

1. Stir together the eggs and yogurt, and pour into the top of a double boiler, or a bowl placed over a saucepan of hot (not boiling) water.

2. Add the cayenne pepper and stir the mixture as it is gently heated. Do not allow to boil.

3. After about 8 minutes, the sauce will thicken. Turn it at once into a warmed serving dish. Garnish if liked with soya (soy) 'bacon' bits. Place in the centre of a large plate and surround with a mixture of raw vegetables. Croûtons also go well with this dip, as does wholemeal French bread.

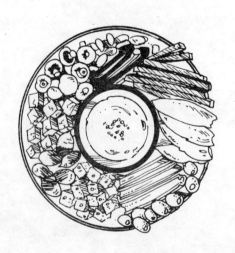

SWISS CHEESE FONDUE

Imperial (Metric)	American
1 clove garlic	1 clove garlic
½ pint (285ml) dry white wine	1⅓ cups dry white wine
1 lb (455g) Gruyère cheese	4 cups Gruyère cheese
2 teaspoons cornflour	2 teaspoons cornstarch
Pinch of nutmeg	Pinch of nutmeg
Seasoning to taste	Seasoning to taste
2 tablespoons Kirsch or brandy (optional)	2 tablespoons Kirsch or brandy (optional)

1. Cut the garlic and rub it around the inside of a fondue pan, heavy casserole or heatproof dish.

2. Pour in all but 2 tablespoons of the wine and heat gently to boiling point.

3. Add the grated cheese and continue heating, stirring continually, until the cheese melts.

4. Mix the cornflour (cornstarch) with the remaining wine and add to the pan. Simmer 5 minutes more, still stirring continually. Add nutmeg and seasoning. Stir in the Kirsch or brandy for a more exotic flavour.

5. Serve the fondue from the pan in which it has been cooked, if possible over a burner to keep it hot. Stir frequently.

6. Accompany cheese fondue with one or more of the following: wholemeal bread cubes, croûtons, lightly cooked vegetables such as young carrots and asparagus.

VEGETABLE FONDUE

Imperial (Metric)	American
4 oz (115g) sweetcorn	2/3 cup sweetcorn
2 oz (55g) polyunsaturated margarine	1/4 cup polyunsaturated margarine
1/2 small onion	1/2 small onion
1/2 small red pepper	1/2 small red pepper
2 oz (55g) mushrooms	1 cup mushrooms
1/2 pint (285ml) vegetable stock	1 1/3 cups vegetable stock
1 lb (455g) grated Gouda or Cheddar cheese	4 cups grated Gouda or Cheddar cheese
2 teaspoons cornflour	2 teaspoons cornstarch
Pinch of dry mustard	Pinch of dry mustard
Pinch of nutmeg	Pinch of nutmeg
Seasoning to taste	Seasoning to taste
1 tablespoon chopped parsley	1 tablespoon chopped parsley

1. Cook the sweetcorn in water until tender, then drain well.

2. Melt the margarine in a fondue pan, heavy casserole or heatproof dish, tipping it so that the sides are coated.

3. Chop the onion, pepper and cleaned mushrooms and add to the pan. Cook gently until soft.

4. Pour in most of the vegetable stock and bring to the boil.

5. Add the cheese, stirring until it is completely melted.

6. Blend the cornflour (cornstarch) with the remaining vegetable stock, and add to the fondue with the mustard, nutmeg, seasoning, parsley and sweetcorn.

7. Cook gently, stirring all the time, for five minutes more.

8. Serve the fondue from the fondue pan, if possible standing it over a burner so that it stays hot. Stir frequently.

GADO GADO (HOT PEANUT DIP)

Imperial (Metric)	American
1 large onion	1 large onion
2 tablespoons vegetable oil	2 tablespoons vegetable oil
2 cloves garlic, crushed	2 cloves garlic, crushed
¼ pint (140ml) water	⅔ cup water
½ lb (225g) peanut butter	8 ounces peanut butter
Pinch of raw cane sugar	Pinch of raw cane sugar
Squeeze of lemon juice	Squeeze of lemon juice
1 bay leaf, crushed	1 bay leaf, crushed
½ teaspoon ground ginger	½ teaspoon ground ginger
½ teaspoon cayenne pepper	½ teaspoon cayenne pepper
Soya sauce	Soy sauce
Approximately ½ pint (285ml) milk	1⅓ cups milk
Seasoning to taste	Seasoning to taste

1. Chop the onion and fry it in the oil for a few minutes. Add the garlic and continue cooking until the onion becomes translucent.

2. Add the water and, when it boils, add the peanut butter and stir well so that it dissolves.

3. Flavour with the sugar, lemon juice, bay leaf, spices and soya (soy) sauce. Cook gently 5 minutes more.

4. Add enough milk to make a pouring sauce. Warm through, stirring continually.

5. Transfer the sauce to a warmed bowl. Serve at once, with raw vegetables and croûtons for dipping.

5.

MOUSSES AND MOULDS

CURRIED CHEESE MOUSSE
Serves 4

Imperial (Metric)	American
½ lb (225g) curd cheese	1 cup curd cheese
1 tablespoon vegetable oil	1 tablespoon vegetable oil
½ small onion, finely chopped	½ small onion, finely chopped
½ clove garlic, crushed	½ clove garlic, crushed
2 tablespoons cold water	2 tablespoons cold water
2 level teaspoons agar-agar	2 level teaspoons agar-agar
½ pint (285ml) light vegetable stock	1⅓ cups light vegetable stock
½-1 teaspoon curry powder	½-1 teaspoon curry powder
Good pinch of coriander	Good pinch of cilantro
Seasoning of taste	Seasoning of taste
Cucumber to garnish	Cucumber to garnish

1. Cream the cheese to soften it.

2. Heat the oil in a frying pan, and gently sauté the finely chopped onion with the garlic until both begin to soften.

3. Whisk the agar-agar into the water, then pour it into the pan with the vegetable stock.

4. Bring the mixture to the boil, stirring continually, then lower heat and cook a few minutes more. Set aside to cool.

5. Mix the cheese into the other ingredients, either using a fork, or in a blender. Add the curry powder, coriander (cilantro) and seasoning.

6. Spoon into four ramekins and, when cool, place in a refrigerator. Leave until completely set before serving garnished with wafer thin slices of cucumber.

ASPARAGUS MOUSSE

Imperial (Metric)
12 asparagus spears, cooked*
1 pint (570ml) light vegetable stock
2 teaspoons agar-agar
6 oz (170g) low-fat soft cheese
Pinch of paprika
Seasoning to taste

American
12 asparagus spears, cooked*
2½ cups light vegetable stock
2 teaspoons agar-agar
¾ cup low-fat soft cheese
Pinch of paprika
Seasoning to taste

1. Rinse a medium-sized plain mould in cold water. Arrange the asparagus spears across the base so that they radiate out from the centre like spokes on a wheel. Trim as necessary, reserving any extra pieces.

2. Heat the vegetable stock in a saucepan, then whisk in the agar-agar and continue cooking for a few minutes more, whisking continually. Cool slightly.

3. Beat the cheese until smooth, then add it to the vegetable stock and mix well. Add paprika and seasoning, plus any extra asparagus pieces, chopped finely.

4. Pour the mixture gently into the mould. Leave to cool completely, then put into the refrigerator. Leave for about 2 hours, until set.

5. To remove from the mould, dip it quickly into hot water, then invert over a flat serving plate.

* These can be fresh, frozen or tinned.

EGG MOUSSE
Serves 4

Imperial (Metric)	American
3 eggs	3 eggs
¼ pint (140ml) whipping cream	⅔ cup whipping cream
Soya sauce	Soy sauce
Seasoning to taste	Seasoning to taste
1-2 spring onions	1-2 scallions
Watercress to garnish	Watercress to garnish

1. Hard boil the eggs then set aside to cool.

2. Remove the yolks and mash well. Chop the egg whites.

3. Whip the cream until it holds its shape, then mix in the eggs, soya (soy) sauce and seasoning to taste.

4. Chop the onions as fine as possible and add to the other ingredients, making sure they are evenly distributed.

5. Divide the mixture between four ramekins and chill well before serving. Garnish with sprigs of watercress.

AVOCADO NUT MOUSSE
Serves 4

Imperial (Metric)	American
2 large ripe avocados	2 large ripe avocados
1 tablespoon lemon juice	1 tablespoon lemon juice
1 oz (30g) polyunsaturated margarine	2½ tablespoons polyunsaturated margarine
1 oz (30g) wholemeal flour	¼ cup wholewheat flour
⅓ pint (200ml) milk	¾ cup milk
1½ teaspoons agar-agar	1½ teaspoons agar-agar
3 tablespoons cold water	3 tablespoons cold water
2 teaspoons white wine vinegar	2 teaspoons white wine vinegar
4 oz (115g) cottage cheese	½ cup cottage cheese
Soya sauce	Soy sauce
Seasoning to taste	Seasoning to taste
2 oz (55g) coarsely chopped Brazil nuts	½ cup coarsely chopped Brazil nuts

1. Peel the avocados, remove the stones. Mash the flesh together with the lemon juice.

2. Melt the margarine in a saucepan, sprinkle in the flour and cook gently for a few minutes.

3. Add the milk and cook to make a sauce.

4. Whisk the agar-agar into the cold water and then add to the sauce. Bring it to the boil, then lower heat and simmer for a few minutes. Cool slightly.

5. Add the puréed avocados together with the wine vinegar.

6. Sieve the cottage cheese so that it is smooth, then add this to the mixture. Flavour with a little soya (soy) sauce, and seasoning to taste.

7. Add most of the coarsely chopped Brazil nuts.

8. Rinse a serving dish, or four ramekins, with cold water, then spoon in the mixture. Leave to cool, then place in the refrigerator to set firm.

9. Sprinkle with the remaining nuts before serving.

SPICY CAULIFLOWER MOUSSE

Imperial (Metric)
2 tablespoons vegetable oil
1 onion
¾ teaspoon coriander
¾ teaspoon turmeric
Good pinch of dry mustard
Good pinch of cayenne pepper
1 medium cauliflower
Approximately ¼ pint (140ml) cold
  water
⅓ pint (200ml) natural yogurt
The white of a large egg
Seasoning to taste
Crisp fried onion to garnish

American
2 tablespoons vegetable oil
1 onion
¾ teaspoon cilantro
¾ teaspoon turmeric
Good pinch of dry mustard
Good pinch of cayenne pepper
1 medium cauliflower
Approximately ⅔ cup cold water
¾ cup plain yogurt
The white of a large egg
Seasoning to taste
Crisp fried onion to garnish

1. Heat the oil in a large pan. Add the sliced onion and cook gently for 5 minutes, or until it begins to soften.

2. Add the spices, stir well, and cook a few minutes more.

3. Break the cauliflower into florets and stir into the spices. Add the water, cover the pan, and cook until the cauliflower is very soft, adding a drop more water if necessary. Cool slightly.

4. Drain the cauliflower and onion if necessary, then purée or mash to a smooth paste.

5. Add the yogurt.

6. Whisk the egg white until stiff then fold gently into the cauliflower and yogurt mixture. Adjust seasoning.

7. Spoon into ramekins and chill briefly. Serve garnished with crisp fried onion.

CUCUMBER CUMIN MOUSSE

Imperial (Metric)
¾ pint (425ml) light vegetable stock
2 teaspoons agar-agar
4 oz (115g) cottage cheese
⅛ pint (70ml) natural yogurt
½ small onion
Approximately ½ teaspoon ground
   cumin, or to taste
Seasoning to taste
1 cucumber

American
2 cups light vegetable stock
2 teaspoons agar-agar
½ cup cottage cheese
½ cup plain yogurt
½ small onion
Approximately ½ teaspoon ground
   cumin, or to taste
Seasoning to taste
1 cucumber

1. Bring the vegetable stock to a gentle boil. Whisk in the agar-agar, and then cook a few minutes more, whisking continually. Set aside to cool.

2. Mash the cottage cheese and mix together with the yogurt (or combine them in a blender).

3. Finely chop the onion and add to the cheese mixture, then stir into the vegetable stock, mixing well. Add cumin and seasoning to taste.

4. Finely slice the cucumber. Rinse a one-pint ring mould with cold water. Arrange slices of the cucumber evenly across the base, and pour in just enough of the jelly to cover them.

5. Stand the mould in a bowl of iced water and leave to set.

6. Arrange more slices of cucumber around the outer edge of the mould and carefully pour in more jelly (if it has begun to set, heat it very gently first).

7. Stand the mould once again in iced water.

8. Repeat once more so that the mould is completely lined with the cucumber slices.

9. Cool to room temperature, then place the mould in the fridge for 1½-2 hours, or until set firm.

10. To release the jelly, dip the mould quickly in hot water, then invert it over a plate. Serve at once.

CAMEMBERT CREAMS
Serves 4

Imperial (Metric)	American
1 small ripe Camembert cheese	1 small ripe Camembert cheese
2 oz (55g) Ricotta or low-fat cream cheese	¼ cup Ricotta or low-fat cream cheese
4 tablespoons whipping cream	4 tablespoons whipping cream
Parsley to garnish	Parsley to garnish

1. Trim the rind from the Camembert cheese, then cut it into small pieces.

2. Mash the two cheeses together until smooth. (If you prefer to do this in a processor, you can add a spoonful or two of milk to help.)

3. Lightly whip the cream. Stir into the cheeses.

4. Spoon into four small ramekins and chill well. Garnish with chopped parsley.

EGG AND TOMATO MOULD

Imperial (Metric)	American
1 pint (570ml) good quality tomato sauce	2½ cups good quality tomato sauce
Soya sauce	Soy sauce
2 teaspoons agar-agar	2 teaspoons agar-agar
Grated rind and juice of ½ lemon	Grated rind and juice of ½ lemon
3 hard-boiled eggs	3 hard-boiled eggs
Watercress to garnish	Watercress to garnish

1. Gently heat the tomato sauce, and sprinkle with soya (soy) sauce.

2. Whisk in the agar-agar, and continue heating and whisking for a few minutes more. Add the lemon rind and juice.

3. Rince a one-pint ring mould in cold water. Arrange the sliced hard-boiled eggs around it. Pour in the tomato mixture.

4. Leave to cool to room temperature, then place in the refrigerator for 2 hours, or until completely set.

5. To release the jelly, dip the mould quickly into hot water, then invert it over a plate.

6. Serve at once, filling the centre with watercress.

RUSSIAN SALAD RING

Imperial (Metric)	American
2 carrots	2 carrots
1 stick celery	1 stalk celery
1 large potato	1 large potato
6 oz (170g) peas	1 cup peas
2 gherkins, chopped	2 gherkins, chopped
½ pint (285ml) light vegetable stock	1⅓ cups light vegetable stock
2 teaspoons agar-agar	2 teaspoons agar-agar
¼ pint (140ml) mayonnaise	⅔ cup mayonnaise
1 tablespoon of lemon juice	1 tablespoon of lemon juice
Seasoning to taste	Seasoning to taste
Cress to garnish	Cress to garnish

1. Peel and cube the carrots; slice the celery; peel and cube the potato.

2. Cook the prepared vegetables, plus the peas, until just tender. Drain well. Stir together, and add the chopped gherkins.

3. In a saucepan heat the vegetable stock gently, then whisk in the agar-agar. Continue heating and whisking for a few minutes more, then set aside to cool.

4. Stir the vegetables into the stock. Add the mayonnaise, lemon juice and a generous amount of seasoning.

5. Rinse a one-pint ring mould in cold water. Pour in the mixture and leave to reach room temperature.

6. Chill in the refrigerator until completely set.

7. When ready to serve, dip the mould quickly in hot water and invert it over a plate. Drop some fresh cress into the centre to garnish the ring.

SPINACH RAMEKINS
Serves 4

Imperial (Metric)	American
1 oz (30g) polyunsaturated margarine	2½ tablespoons polyunsaturated margarine
½ clove garlic, crushed	½ clove garlic, crushed
½ onion, chopped	½ onion, chopped
1 lb (455g) spinach	1 pound spinach
1 tablespoon lemon juice	1 tablespoon lemon juice
4 oz (115g) cream cheese	½ cup cream cheese
Good pinch of nutmeg	Good pinch of nutmeg
Seasoning to taste	Seasoning to taste
Soya 'bacon' bits to garnish	Soy *Bac-O-Bits* to garnish

1. Melt the margarine in a large pan and fry the garlic and chopped onion for 5 minutes.

2. Add the washed, shredded spinach, stir, cover the pan and cook for 8-10 minutes, or until the spinach is soft.

3. Drain the mixture well, then purée.

4. Add the lemon juice, cream cheese, nutmeg and seasoning, mixing well. (This can be done by hand or in a blender.)

5. Divide between four ramekins, smooth the top. Chill well. Serve sprinkled with 'bacon' bits.

TOMATO CHEESE MOULDS WITH OLIVES

Imperial (Metric)
1/3 pint (200ml) tomato juice
1 tablespoon lemon juice
1½ teaspoons agar-agar
4 oz (115g) grated Cheddar cheese
Chopped parsley
Soya sauce
Seasoning to taste
12 stuffed green olives
Shredded lettuce to serve

American
¾ cup tomato juice
1 tablespoon lemon juice
1½ teaspoons agar-agar
1 cup grated Cheddar cheese
Chopped parsley
Soy sauce
Seasoning to taste
12 stuffed green olives
Shredded lettuce to serve

1. Put the tomato juice and lemon juice into a saucepan and bring slowly to the boil.

2. Whisk in the agar-agar and continue heating, whisking at the same time, for 2 or 3 minutes more.

3. Remove from the heat and cool briefly, then stir in the cheese so that it melts.

4. Add the parsley, soya (soy) sauce and seasoning. Leave to cool to room temperature.

5. Slice the olives and arrange across the base of four or more (depending on size) individual moulds. Pour in the mixture. Chill for 1½-2 hours, or until set.

6. To serve, dip the moulds quickly into hot water, then slide out onto a plate. Serve on a bed of shredded lettuce.

WALDORF SALAD

Imperial (Metric)	American
3 sticks celery	3 stalks celery
2 apples	2 apples
1 large banana	1 large banana
8 dates	8 dates
3 oz (85g) walnut pieces	²/₃ cup English walnut pieces
1 tablespoon lemon juice	1 tablespoon lemon juice
¾ pint (425ml) white grape juice	2 cups white grape juice
2 teaspoons agar-agar	2 teaspoons agar-agar
Endive to serve	Endive to serve

1. Wash and chop the celery. Core and dice the apples. Slice the banana. Chop the dates.

2. Mix the prepared ingredients with the walnut pieces and toss in the lemon juice.

3. Pour the grape juice into a saucepan and bring gently to the boil. Whisk in the agar-agar, and cook for a few minutes more, whisking the mixture all the time. Set aside to cool.

4. Rinse a medium-sized plain or decorated mould with cold water.

5. Stir the celery, fruit and nuts into the cooled grape juice and leave until it begins to thicken, then pour into the mould.

6. When the mixture reaches room temperature, stir once more to distribute the ingredients evenly. Then place in a refrigerator and leave for 1½-2 hours, or until set firm.

7. When ready to serve the salad, dip the mould quickly into hot water, then invert over a serving plate. Surround with crisp endive leaves before taking it to the table.

PEANUT AND CELERY MOULD

Imperial (Metric)
5 oz (140g) smooth peanut butter
1/2 pint (285ml) vegetable stock
2 level teaspoons agar-agar
Good squeeze of lemon juice
1 stick celery
2-3 tablespoons cream or top of the
    milk
Pinch of chilli powder
Seasoning to taste
Celery leaves to garnish
Salted peanuts to garnish

American
Good 1/2 cup smooth peanut butter
1 1/3 cups vegetable stock
2 level teaspoons agar-agar
Good squeeze of lemon juice
1 stalk celery
2-3 tablespoons cream or half and
    half
Pinch of chili powder
Seasoning to taste
Celery leaves to garnish
Salted peanuts to garnish

1. Beat the peanut butter until creamy.

2. Put the stock into a saucepan and bring gently to the boil.

3. Whisk in the agar-agar and continue cooking, whisking continually, for a few minutes more.

4. Take the pan off the heat, add the peanut butter and lemon juice, and blend until completely dissolved.

5. Chop the celery as fine as possible, and add to the peanut mixture.

6. Stir in just enough cream to give a smooth texture, and light colour. Add chilli powder and seasoning to taste.

7. Rinse a small plain or decorated mould with cold water.

8. Pour in the peanut and celery mixture and leave to cool to room temperature.

9. Put into a refrigerator and leave to set completely — if the celery is not evenly distributed, stir the mixture as the jelly begins to set.

10. To remove from the mould, dip it quickly in hot water, then invert over a serving plate. Garnish with celery leaves and some chopped salted peanuts.

HOT CARROT RAMEKINS
Serves 4

Imperial (Metric)
1 lb (455g) carrots
Approximately ½ pint (285ml)
  vegetable stock
4 oz (115g) grated Edam cheese
2 eggs, beaten
Seasoning to taste
Good pinch of dried marjoram
½ oz (15g) polyunsaturated
  margarine
1 oz (30g) wholemeal breadcrumbs
Parsley to garnish

American
1 pound carrots
1⅓ cups vegetable stock
½ cup grated Edam cheese
2 eggs, beaten
Seasoning to taste
Good pinch of dried marjoram
1 good tablespoon polyunsaturated
  margarine
½ cup wholewheat breadcrumbs
Parsley to garnish

1. Peel and chop the carrots. Cook in the vegetable stock until tender, then drain well.

2. Purée the carrots, and drain again. Put into a bowl.

3. Stir in the grated cheese, add the beaten eggs, seasoning and marjoram.

4. Lightly grease four ramekins and spoon some of the mixture into each.

5. Bake at 375°F/190°C (Gas Mark 5) for about 20 minutes, or until set.

6. Meanwhile melt the margarine and fry the breadcrumbs until crisp and brown. Sprinkle them over the ramekins before serving, and garnish with sprigs of parsley.

WATERCRESS MOUSSE

Imperial (Metric)	**American**
¼ pint (140ml) light vegetable stock	⅔ cup light vegetable stock
1½ teaspoons agar-agar	1½ teaspoons agar-agar
2 tablespoons lemon juice	2 tablespoons lemon juice
4 oz (115g) Boursin or other soft herbed cheese	½ cup Boursin or other soft herbed cheese
¼ pint (140ml) soured cream	⅔ cup soured cream
Approximately ½ bunch watercress	Approximately ½ bunch watercress
1 tablespoon chopped parsley	1 tablespoon chopped parsley
Seasoning to taste	Seasoning to taste
Lettuce and tomatoes to serve	Lettuce and tomatoes to serve

1. Put the stock into a saucepan, heat gently, whisk in the agar-agar. Continue heating for a few minutes more. Add the lemon juice, then set aside to cool.

2. Mash the cheese together with the soured cream.

3. Wash, trim and chop the watercress.

4. Mix together the cheese and watercress, and stir into the vegetable stock, blending them thoroughly. Add the parsley and seasoning.

5. Rinse 4 small moulds with cold water, then fill each one with some of the mixture. Leave to cool to room temperature.

6. Chill in the refrigerator until completely set.

7. Dip each mould quickly into hot water, then invert over a plate. Serve on a bed of lettuce and tomato slices.

6.
ACCOMPANIMENTS

CRUDITÉS (RAW VEGETABLES)

Imperial (Metric)
About 1 lb (455g) mixed vegetables
such as carrots, celery, peppers,
fennel, spring onions, young green
beans, cherry tomatoes,
cauliflower florets, etc.

American
About 1 pound mixed vegetables
such as carrots, celery, peppers,
fennel, scallions, young green
beans, cherry tomatoes,
cauliflower florets, etc.

1. Pick the freshest, most tender vegetables available.

2. Prepare them shortly before you intend to serve them.

3. Ingredients such as carrots, peppers and fennel are best cut into
   strips. Spring onions (scallions), green beans and celery need to be
   cleaned and trimmed.

4. Arrange them attractively, taking their colours and shapes into
   consideration. Crudités can be lightly chilled before being served.

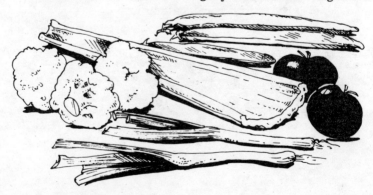

CROÛTONS

Imperial (Metric)	American
4 thick slices wholemeal bread	4 thick slices wholewheat bread
1 tablespoon vegetable oil	1 tablespoon vegetable oil
2 oz (55g) polyunsaturated margarine or butter*	¼ cup polyunsaturated margarine or butter*

1. Trim the crusts from the bread, then cut into even-sized cubes.

2. Heat the oil together with the fat and, when hot, add the cubes of bread.

3. Fry for a few minutes, stirring frequently, until the croûtons are crisp and brown on the outside.

4. Drain well, and serve warm or cold. Croûtons should be speared with a small fork or cocktail stick, and can then be dipped.

*For those who are not too concerned about cutting their consumption of saturated fats, butter does give a better flavour.

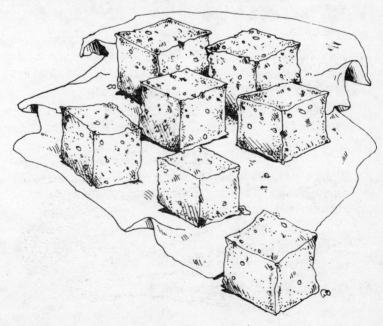

GARLIC CROÛTONS

Imperial (Metric)
4 thick slices wholemeal bread
1 tablespoon vegetable oil
2 oz (55g) polyunsaturated
  margarine or butter*
1 clove garlic, crushed

American
4 thick slices wholewheat bread
1 tablespoon vegetable oil
¼ cup polyunsaturated margarine or
  butter*
1 clove garlic, crushed

1.   Trim the crusts from the bread, then cut into even-sized cubes.

2.   Heat the oil together with the fat, and gently fry the garlic for a
     few minutes at least.

3.   Discard the garlic.

4.   Fry the bread cubes in the flavoured fat, stirring them frequently
     so that they are crisp and brown on all sides.

5.   Drain well. Serve warm or cold, speared with a fork or cocktail stick.
     Use with dips.

*See note under Croûtons (page 91).

MELBA TOAST

Imperial (Metric)
8 medium slices stale wholemeal
  bread

American
8 medium slices stale wholewheat
  bread

1.   Toast the slices lightly on both sides.

2.   Whilst toast is still warm, remove the crusts. Use a sharp knife to
     halve each slice. Then carefully cut down the length of the toast
     to make wafer-thin slices.

3.   Arrange these on a baking sheet. Place in a hot oven 400°F/200°C
     (Gas Mark 6) for just a few minutes until the toast begins to curl
     and is a rich brown in colour.

4.   Cool, and store in an airtight container.

BREAD STICKS

Imperial (Metric)
1 oz (30g) fresh yeast
Approx. 1/3 pint (200ml) warm water
10 oz (285g) wholemeal flour
Good pinch of salt
Egg and milk to glaze
Coarse sea salt or sesame seeds to
  coat

American
2 1/2 tablespoons fresh yeast
Approx. 3/4 cup warm water
2 1/2 cups wholewheat flour
Good pinch of salt
Egg and milk to glaze
Coarse sea salt or sesame seeds to
  coat

1. Mix the yeast in a few tablespoons of the warm water. When dissolved set aside.

2. Sift together the flour and salt. When the yeast mixture begins to froth, add it to the flour with enough warm water to make a soft dough.

3. Turn onto a lightly floured board, and knead for at least a few minutes, until smooth and glossy.

4. Place the dough in a warmed bowl, cover, and leave in a warm place for 1 hour, or until doubled in size.

5. Break off pieces of dough and roll out to thin rectangles.

6. With a floured knife, cut these into strips about 1 inch (2.5cm) wide, and then roll them into sticks.

7. Place on greased baking sheets, leaving a little space between each one. Beat together an egg and some milk, and brush the sticks with the mixture.

8. Set aside in a warm spot to double in size.

9. Brush lightly with more of the egg and milk mixture, and then sprinkle with salt or sesame seeds.

10. Bake at 400°F/200°C (Gas Mark 6) for 15-20 minutes, or until crisp. Cool, then store in an airtight tin.

SESAME SNAPS

Imperial (Metric)	American
1-2 spring onions	1-2 scallions
½ lb (225g) wholemeal flour	2 cups wholewheat flour
4 oz (115g) sesame seeds	¾ cup sesame seeds
Seasoning to taste	Seasoning to taste
Cold water to mix	Cold water to mix
Vegetable oil for frying	Vegetable oil for frying

1. Chop the onions as fine as possible.

2. Mix together the flour, seeds, seasoning and chopped onion, then stir in just enough cold water to make a dough. Knead until pliable.

3. On a floured board roll out the dough. Cut into even sized strips.

4. Heat the oil in a saucepan and, when hot, drop in the strips and deep fry until golden and crisp.

5. Drain well on paper towels and serve whilst still warm, or store in an airtight container until needed.

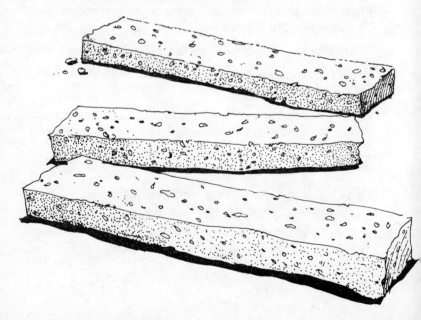

BRAN FINGERS

Imperial (Metric)
3 oz (85g) wholemeal flour
1 oz (30g) bran
Sea salt
2 oz (55g) polyunsaturated
  margarine
Approximately 2 tablespoons milk
Extra bran for rolling out

American
¾ cup wholewheat flour
¼ cup bran
Sea salt
¼ cup polyunsaturated margarine
Approximately 2 tablespoons milk
Extra bran for rolling out

1. Sift together the flour, bran and sea salt.

2. Rub in the margarine to make a crumb-like mixture.

3. Stir in just enough milk to bind to a firm dough.

4. Knead the dough lightly, then wrap in clingfilm and chill briefly.

5. Roll out the dough on a board covered with bran. Shape it into a rectangle. Cut in half.

6. Transfer to a greased baking sheet. Mark into fingers, and prick to pattern.

7. Bake at 400°F/200°C (Gas Mark 6) for about 15 minutes. Cool slightly on the tray, then break carefully into fingers and transfer to a wire rack.

8. When completely cold, store in an airtight tin.

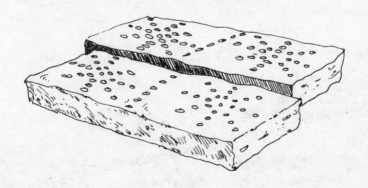

CHEESE STRAWS

Imperial (Metric)
4 oz (115g) wholemeal flour
Good pinch of mustard powder
Good pinch of paprika
Seasoning to taste
2 oz (55g) polyunsaturated
  margarine
2 oz (55g) Cheddar cheese
1 egg yolk
Cold water
Milk to glaze

American
1 cup wholewheat flour
Good pinch of mustard powder
Good pinch of paprika
Seasoning to taste
¼ cup polyunsaturated margarine
½ cup Cheddar cheese
1 egg yolk
Cold water
Milk to glaze

1. Sieve together the flour, spices and seasoning.

2. Use fingertips to rub in the margarine lightly.

3. Grate the cheese and add to the mixture.

4. Stir in the egg yolk with just enough cold water to bind the ingredients into a dough. Knead this briefly.

5. Roll onto a floured board to about ¼ inch (5mm) thickness. Cut into narrow strips and twist each one before placing on a lightly-greased baking sheet. Brush with milk.

6. Bake at 400°F/200°C (Gas Mark 6) for 10-15 minutes. Cool briefly on the sheet before transferring carefully to a wire rack. Leave to cool. Store in an airtight container.

BLUE CHEESE BISCUITS

Imperial (Metric)
4 oz (115g) blue cheese
4 oz (115g) polyunsaturated
  margarine
½ lb (225g) wholemeal flour
2 level teaspoons baking powder

American
1 cup blue cheese
½ cup polyunsaturated margarine
2 cups wholewheat flour
2 level teaspoons baking soda

1. Crumble the cheese into a mixing bowl.

2. Use a fork to mix in the margarine and then the flour.

3. Turn the dough onto a board and knead until smooth and elastic.
    Wrap in clingfilm and chill for 30 minutes.

4. Roll the dough out thinly, then use a sharp knife to cut in fingers
    (or cut into rounds if you prefer). Arrange on a lightly-greased baking
    sheet.

5. Bake at 425°F/220°C (Gas Mark 7) for 10 minutes or until golden
    and crisp. Cool the biscuits, then store them in an airtight container
    until needed.

OATMEAL BISCUITS

Imperial (Metric)
4 oz (115g) wholemeal flour
3 oz (85g) oatmeal
Pinch of sea salt
2 oz (55g) polyunsaturated
  margarine

American
1 cup wholewheat flour
¾ cup oatmeal
Pinch of sea salt
¼ cup polyunsaturated margarine

1. Mix together the flour and oatmeal, add the sea salt.

2. Rub the fat into the dry ingredients until the mixture resembles
    crumbs.

3. Add just enough cold water to bind the flour and oats. Knead briefly,
    then roll out on a lightly-floured board.

4. Use a cutter or glass to shape into small circles. Arrange these on
    a greased baking sheet.

5. Cook in an oven heated to 400°F/200°C (Gas Mark 6) for about
    20 minutes, or until crisp and brown. Cool on a wire rack and, when
    completely cold, store in an airtight container.

TORTILLAS

Imperial (Metric)
½ lb (225g) maize flour
Good pinch of salt
¼ teaspoon chilli powder, or to taste
½ pint (285ml) warm water

American
1½ cups cornmeal
Good pinch of salt
¼ teaspoon chili powder, or to taste
1⅓ cups warm water

1. Sift together the maize flour (cornmeal), salt and chilli powder.

2. Gradually add the water, mixing well to make a soft dough.

3. Break into even-sized pieces and roll out (between clingfilm, if necessary — it can be sticky). You should have about twelve saucer-like circles.

4. Heat a heavy based frying pan. When hot, place a tortilla in the pan and cook over a medium heat for a few minutes, until browned underneath. Turn and cook the other side.

5. Keep the tortilla warm, and cook the rest in the same way.

Note: Tortillas can also be deep fried, which makes them even more crisp in texture. Leave them in the fat for little more than a minute, and drain on paper towels before serving.

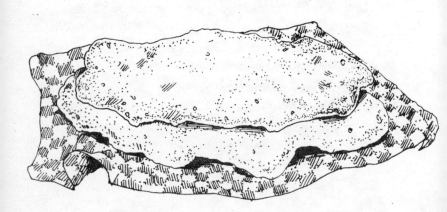

HOME-MADE POTATO CRISPS

Imperial (Metric)
½ lb (225g) potatoes
Vegetable oil for frying

American
8 ounces potatoes
Vegetable oil for frying

1. Scrub and then peel the potatoes. Slice very thinly into rounds.

2. Heat the oil until very hot.

3. Drop in the potato slices a few at a time, and cook, shaking frequently, until browned.

4. Drain well and serve warm or cold. Home-made crisps are best eaten when fresh.

POTATOES FOR DIPPING

Imperial (Metric)
1 lb (455g) tiny new potatoes
Sprig of mint

American
1 pound tiny new potatoes
Sprig of mint

1. Choose the smallest possible potatoes — about the size of a walnut, or smaller still.

2. Scrub the potatoes, but do not peel.

3. Steam them with the mint until just cooked — they should still be firm in texture.

4. Drain well, then rub off the skin if you prefer them that way. (The skins, can, of course, be left on.)

5. Serve the potatoes hot, warm or cold. Spear each one with a small fork or cocktail stick and use with dips.

DEEP-FRIED MUSHROOMS

Imperial (Metric)
½ lb (225g) button mushrooms
2 oz (55g) wholemeal flour
1 egg
2 oz (55g) fine dried wholemeal
    breadcrumbs
Vegetable oil for frying

American
3 cups button mushrooms
½ cup wholewheat flour
1 egg
½ cup fine dried wholewheat
    breadcrumbs
Vegetable oil for frying

1. Wipe the mushrooms clean.

2. Dip each one first into the flour, then the beaten egg, then the breadcrumbs, making sure they are well and evenly coated.

3. Heat the oil until a cube of bread dropped into it will brown in just under a minute.

4. Deep fry the mushrooms a few at a time, until crisp and golden. Drain well. Serve whilst still warm, and with small forks or cocktail sticks to hold them for dipping.

FRENCH BREAD

Imperial (Metric)
½ pint (285ml) water and milk,
    warmed
1 teaspoon raw brown sugar or
    honey
¾ oz (20g) fresh yeast
1 lb (455g) 81 per cent wholemeal
    flour*
Good pinch of salt
2 oz (55g) polyunsaturated
    margarine or butter

American
1⅓ cups water and milk, warmed
1 teaspoon raw brown sugar or
    honey
Just under 2 tablespoons fresh yeast
4 cups 81 per cent wholewheat
    flour*
Good pinch of salt
¼ cup polyunsaturated margarine or
    butter

1. Make a paste by stirring a drop of the liquid with the sugar and yeast. Add to the rest of the liquid and set aside in a warm, draught-free spot.

2. Sift together the flour and salt. Add the yeast mixture as soon as it begins to froth, and make a dough.

3. Turn the dough out onto a floured board, and knead well until smooth and elastic.

4. Melt the fat and use a little of it to grease a warm bowl. Put in the dough, cover, and leave in a warm spot for about an hour, until doubled in size.

5. On a floured board, knock back the dough, then knead again. Return it to the warm lightly-greased bowl, and leave to double in size again.

6. Knead briefly, then mould the dough into the traditional French bread stick (or make two smaller sticks). Put onto a greased baking sheet, and set aside in a warm spot to rise.

7. When well risen, brush the bread with the remaining fat. Bake in a pre-heated oven at 425°F/220°C (Gas Mark 7) for about 20 minutes, or until well coloured.

* French bread is traditionally made with white flour, so this loaf will be coarser in texture — though not as heavy as bread made with 100 per cent wholemeal flour (81 per cent has had the bran removed). You can, in fact, make the bread with any one of these flours, though the end result will vary.

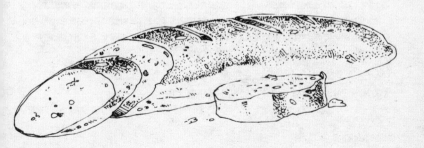

PITTA BREAD

Imperial (Metric)	American
½ lb (225g) wholemeal flour	2 cups wholewheat flour
Good pinch of salt	Good pinch of salt
¼ pint (140ml) warm water	⅔ cup warm water
¼ oz (7g) fresh yeast	Good ½ tablespoon fresh yeast
½ teaspoon raw brown sugar or honey	½ teaspoon raw brown sugar or honey
Vegetable oil	Vegetable oil

1. In a bowl sift together the flour and salt.

2. In another bowl add the warm water to the yeast and sugar, stirring well so that they dissolve completely.

3. Leave the mixture in a warm spot for 10 minutes, or until frothy.

4. Add the yeast to the flour to make a dough and knead well until glossy. Lightly oil a warm bowl, add the dough, cover, and leave in a warm spot for 30-40 minutes, or until doubled in size.

5. Knead the dough again for a minute or two, then break it into four even-sized pieces. Roll out to about ¼ inch (5mm) thickness, shaping each piece into an oval.

6. Arrange these on greased baking sheets.

7. Put straight into an oven pre-heated to 400°F/200°C (Gas Mark 6) and cook for about 8-10 minutes, by which time they should be well risen.

8. Cool on a wire rack. Serve warm to be broken into pieces and used to scoop up dips. Cold pitta breads can be halved, then opened up to make a pouch, which can be filled with whatever you fancy — pâté and salad make a good combination.

Note: This amount of dough makes four good sized pitta breads. For parties, you could make eight smaller ones.

CHAPATIS

Imperial (Metric)
½ lb (225g) wholemeal flour
Good pinch of salt
Approximately ¼ pint (140ml) warm
  water

American
2 cups wholewheat flour
Good pinch of salt
Approximately ⅔ cup warm water

1. Sift the flour and salt together into a bowl.

2. Gradually add enough water to make a fairly firm dough, and knead briefly until smooth and glossy.

3. Wrap in clingfilm and chill for 30 minutes.

4. Break the dough into small balls and roll each one out on a floured board to make a thin circle.

5. Heat a heavy frying pan (ungreased) until very hot. Put in a round of dough, and cook gently for half a minute, then press down with a wide spatula.

6. When just beginning to brown underneath turn and cook the second side in the same way. Blisters will appear — they are a distinctive part of chapatis. Keep warm whilst cooking the rest in the same way. Serve warm.

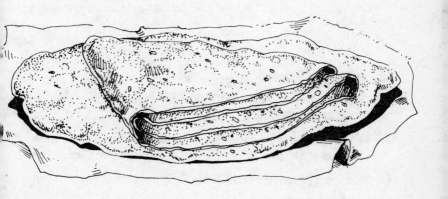

PURIS

Imperial (Metric)
Dough, as for Chapatis (page 103)
Vegetable oil for frying

American
Dough, as for Chapatis (page 103)
Vegetable oil for frying

1. Make up the dough as for chapatis.

2. Lightly grease a board, then roll out small pieces of the dough to make thin circles.

3. In a wide frying pan heat a reasonable amount of oil to a good heat.

4. Drop in a puri, and cook gently, using a slotted spoon to press it down. When it inflates, turn and cook the other side, so that it is lightly browned all over.

5. Remove, drain, and keep the puri warm whilst cooking the rest of the dough in the same way.

PASTRY PUFFS

Imperial (Metric)
¾ pint (425ml) water
2 oz (55g) butter
Good 4 oz (115g) wholemeal flour
Sea salt
3 small eggs
Vegetable oil for frying

American
2 cups water
¼ cup butter
1 cup wholewheat flour
Sea salt
3 small eggs
Vegetable oil for frying

1. Put the water and butter into a saucepan.

2. Sift together the flour and salt.

3. Heat the water and butter to boiling point, then remove from the heat and add the flour.

4. Return the pan to the cooker, and continue heating gently, stirring continually, until the mixture leaves the sides of the pan. Cool slightly.

5. Beat the eggs together and add gradually to the mixture in the pan.

6. Use a spoon to form small balls of dough.

7. Heat a good amount of vegetable oil in a saucepan and drop in the balls one at a time. Cook gently until puffed up and golden.

8. Drain well, and keep the pastry puffs warm whilst using up the rest of the mixture in the same way. Serve at once.

FRUIT FOR DIPS

Imperial (Metric)	American
½ medium cantaloupe melon	½ medium cantaloupe melon
White wine or fruit juice	White wine or fruit juice
2 firm bananas	2 firm bananas
2 apples	2 apples
Good squeeze of lemon juice	Good squeeze of lemon juice

1. Halve the melon and scoop out the flesh with a melon baller. Marinate the melon balls in just enough white wine or juice to cover them, leaving them in the fridge so that they chill at the same time.

.2 Cut the bananas into even-sized chunks; cut each of the unpeeled apples into eight slices. Turn the fruit in lemon juice so that it keeps its colour.

3. Arrange the fruit pieces attractively, and give each diner a small fork or cocktail stick with which to hold and dip the fruit.

Note: Fruit makes a delicious and unusual accompaniment to creamy dips such as Coconut Dip (page 60).

Appendix
MENU IDEAS

Pâtés, dips, mousses — all are ideal when you want something to snack on. But they can also form the basis for a variety of meals to be served to the young and those with more sophisticated tastes, in summer and winter, on just about every occasion. Following are just a few suggestions as to how they can be incorporated into menus.

All dishes marked with an asterisk can be found in this book.

SUMMER PATIO BUFFET
Serves 12

Cucumber Cumin Mousse★
Coconut Dip★ with Fruit For Dips★
Spinach Dip★ with Deep Fried Mushrooms★
Indian Egg Pâté★
Olive Pâté★
Bran Fingers★
Sesame Snaps★
Summer Fruit Crumble with Home-Made Ice Cream

QUICK SNACK LUNCH
Serves 4

Watercress Egg Pâté*
Sunflower and Pepper Pâté*
French Bread*
Crudités*
Fresh Fruit
Wholemeal Muffins

VEGAN PARTY
Serves 8

Tahini and Tofu Dip*
Garlic Croûtons*
Cauliflower and Red Lentil Pâté*
Nutty Soya Pâté*
Curried Vegetable Pâté*
Waldorf Salad*
Melba Toast*
Pitta Bread*
Fresh Fruit Salad with Cashew Cream

CHILDREN'S PARTY
Serves 10

'Sausage' Pâté*
Oatmeal Biscuits*
Chilli Peanut Dip* with Celery Sticks
Egg and Tomato Mould*
Potato Crisps*
Cheese Straws*
Cheese cubes, pieces of fruit and vegetables on sticks
Cakes
Biscuits
Jellies made with agar-agar

CHRISTMAS GET-TOGETHER
Serves 20

Guacamole★ with Pastry Puffs★
Tomato halves and celery sticks filled with Creamy Cheese Pâté★ and
   Chestnut Pâté★
Hummus with Yogurt★
'Pork' and Pepper Terrine★
Cottage Cheese Dip with Caraway★
Asparagus Mousse★
Tortillas★
French Bread★
Blue Cheese Biscuits★
Hot Stuffed Peaches served with yogurt or cream (use dried peach halves)

FONDUE DINNER
Serves 6

Potted Mushrooms with Almonds★
Swiss Cheese Fondue★ with wholemeal bread cubes and croûtons★
Chicory, tomato and walnut salad
Dried Fruit Compote with flaked almonds and sweet biscuits

INDEX

Asparagus Mousse, 77
Aubergine Dip with Tahini, 58
Aubergine Yogurt Dip, 57
Autumn Pâté, 45
Avocado Nut Mousse, 79

Barbecue Dip, 71
Barley and Bean Pâté, 22
Black Bean Pâté, 29
blender/grinder, electric, 9, 10
Blue Cheese Biscuits, 96
Blue Cheese Dip, 52
Bran Fingers, 95
Bread Sticks, 93
Brussels Sprouts Pâté, 28

Camembert Creams, 82
Carrot Ramekins, Hot, 88
Cashew Pâté, 38
Cauliflower and Red Lentil Pâté, 18
Cauliflower Mousse, Spicy, 80
Celery and Blue Cheese Pâté, 32
Chapatis, 103
Cheese Dip, Hot, 70
Cheese Pâté with Olives, 19
Cheese, Potted, 43
Cheese Straws, 96
Cheesy Pineapple Dip, 58
Chestnut Pâté, 34
Chick Pea Pâté, 27
Chilli Peanut Dip, 67
Coconut Dip, 60
Cottage Cheese Dip with Caraway, 54
Creamy Cheese Pâté, 30

Creamy Mousse Dip, 55
Croûtons, 91
Crudités (Raw Vegetables), 90
Cucumber Cumin Mousse, 81
Curd Cheese and 'Bacon' Pâté, 38
Curried Cheese Mousse, 76
Curried Split Pea Pâté, 13
Curried Tofu Dip, 59
Curried Vegetable Pâté, 42

dairy products, 8, 9

Egg and Avocado Pâté, 15
Egg and Tomato Mould, 82
Egg Mousse, 78

Feta Cheese Dip, 68
French Bread, 100
Fruit for Dips, 105

Gado Gado (Hot Peanut Dip), 75
Garlic Croûtons, 92
Garlic Mayonnaise with Pine Nuts, 62
Green Mayonnaise, 63
Gribiche Dip, 65
Guacamole, 50

Hummus with Yogurt, 52

Indian Egg Pâté, 39

Kidney Bean Pâté, 17

Lancashire Dip with Mushrooms, 56

Lentil Dip, 61
Lentil, Nut and Mushroom Terrine,
    47

Melba Toast, 92
menu suggestions
  Children's Party, 108
  Christmas Get-Together, 109
  Fondue Dinner, 109
  Quick Snack Lunch, 108
  Summer Patio Buffet, 107
  Vegan Party, 108
Mixed Vegetable Terrine, 48
Mock Meat Pâté, 24
Mushrooms, Deep Fried, 100
Mushrooms, Potted, with Almonds, 36

Nutty Soya Pâté, 28

Oat and Parsnip Pâté, 14
Oatmeal Biscuits, 97
Olive Pâté, 44

Pastry Puffs, 104
pâté de foie gras, 8
pâté en croute, 7
Pea and Potato Pâté, 25
Peanut and Celery Mould, 87
Peanut Pâté, Quick, 16
Pineapple Hazelnut Pâté, 40
Piquant Avocado Pâté, 33
Pitta Bread, 102
'Pork' and Pepper Terrine, 46
Potato Crisps, Home-made, 99
Potatoes for Dipping, 99
presentation of food, 10, 11
Pumpkin Pâté, 40

Puris, 104

Russian Salad Ring, 83

'Sausage' Pâté, 35
Sesame Snaps, 94
Skordalia, 64
Soya Yeast Pâté, 21
Spinach and Tofu Pâté, 37
Spinach Dip, 53
Spinach Ramekins, 84
Sunflower and Pepper Pâté, 36
Sweet and Sour Bean Pâté, 31
Sweet and Sour Dip with Olives, 69
Sweetcorn Dip, 56
Swiss Cheese Fondue, 73

Tahini and Tofu Dip, 55
Tahini Parsley Pâté, 41
terrines, 8
Tofu Avocado Dip, 51
Tomato Cheese Moulds with Olives,
    85
Tortillas, 98

vegan recipes, 9
Vegetable Dip, 66
Vegetable Fondue, 74
Vegetable Pâté, Raw, 26

Waldorf Salad, 86
Walnut Dip, 51
Walnut Pâté, 20
Watercress Egg Pâté, 23
Watercress Mousse, 89

Yogurt Hollandaise Dip, 72